REDISCOVERING
REVERENCE

MICHAEL L. GOWENS

◆————————◆

Sovereign Grace Publications
Lexington, Kentucky

REDISCOVERING REVERENCE
Published by Sovereign Grace Publications
Post Office Box 23514
Lexington, Kentucky 40523-3514
www.sovgrace.net
sgpublications@insightbb.com

ISBN 978-1-929635-09-2

Scripture quotations are from the *King James Version* of the Bible.

Printed in the United States of America.

Contents

Introduction

Among the one-hundred-fifty great hymn poems Frederick Faber (1814-1863) left as his legacy to Christianity, the following survives as one of his best:

How dread are Thine eternal years,
O Everlasting Lord!
By prostrate spirits day and night
Incessantly adored!
How beautiful, how beautiful
The sight of Thee must be,
Thine endless wisdom, boundless power,
And awful purity!
Oh how I fear Thee, living God!
With deepest, tenderest fears,
And worship Thee with trembling hope
And penitential tears.

Only one of the half-dozen hymnals (from various denominational traditions) on my shelves, however, include the hymn in their collection. Why? Of course, there may be any number of reasons. Perhaps the fact of Faber's secession to Roman Catholicism influenced its omission from many evangelical hymnals. But that seems unlikely since many include other works from his pen such as "Faith of our Fathers" and "There's A Wideness in God's Mercy". Maybe the hymn was omitted because editors determined that the poetry was poor, or the meter was awkward, or the music attached to it was unspectacular. Indeed, there may be many reasons.

But I suspect (granted, this is sheer conjecture) that most editors bypassed it simply because it was not popular. Few churches would sing it. And why wouldn't they sing it? Because the thoughts it conveys were deemed too heavy—its sentiments too somber and foreboding. It speaks of "dread years," "awful purity," "trembling hope," and "penitential tears." Most shocking of all, Faber admits, "Oh how I *fear Thee*, living God."

Fear Thee? Is this the kind of language with which Christian people ordinarily think of God? It's certainly not the kind of expression of worship to God that is common in Christian circles. In fact, I suspect that not a few professed believers today would feel just a little uncomfortable with this concept of "fearing God." Why? I would suggest three primary reasons.

A Natural Antagonism

First, "the fear of the Lord" is a theme that runs cross-grain to the sinful hearts of men. Fallen sinners don't like to think about subjects like this. That's one sign of our sinfulness. Romans 1:28 affirms that man by nature does not "like to retain God in [his] knowledge." He says to God, "Depart from us, for we desire not the knowledge of Thy ways" (Job 21:14).

Poll statistics indicate that the overwhelming majority of people in America confess to a belief "in God," but they are quick to add, "Not the jealous, wrathful, judgmental God of the Old Testament." Rejecting the Biblical concept of God, modern man has fabricated a god for himself that he can live with.

C. S. Lewis put it poignantly: "God created man in His image, and man has returned the favor." The depraved heart of man is hostile to the very idea that God would hold him accountable. He resents Divine restrictions on his thinking and behavior (Ps. 2:1-3). His mind is at enmity with God (Rom. 8:7; Col. 1:21).

The Influence of an Irreverent Society

Secondly, this concept is unpalatable to many Christian people because of the eroding influence of this ungodly world. These are irreverent times. Blatant and overt blasphemy of the name of God and the character of the Lord Jesus Christ from the popular media culture is relentless. Bible believing Christians and the precious truths they believe are fair game on every talk-show, in every editorial, and in every university classroom.

People think nothing today of ridiculing the concepts of a final judgment or taking the Lord's name in vain. They audaciously presume to edit God, discarding and rewording His book according to personal preference. Some are even openly hostile to Him.

The September-October, 1999, issue of the Baptist magazine *Light* includes an article by John Franklin entitled "The Root Cause of America's Moral Collapse." Franklin argues that "the most critical need in our churches and culture today is to recapture a proper understanding of what it means to fear God." He astutely observes that "the trial of President Clinton was not as much about his morality as that of the nation," arguing that "the awareness of our accountability for sin has been lost from modern culture, and America does not fear God…[but] disregards and despises Him."[1]

In some cases, this spirit of cultural irreverence takes the form of actual disdain. In an article from a university newspaper entitled "Christianity, Absurd Religion," the author responds to the idea that a loving God sent His Son to die for sinners:

> What an absurd concept. Think about it. God (an Omnipotent being!), knowingly sends his son to be nailed to a cross to give you eternal life. If God is all-powerful, he

could have given everyone eternal life by his mere whim. If God was all loving and all good, he would not have created someone for the explicit purpose of being murdered just to communicate a message. If I were a loving father, I would not have a son for the specific reason of having his life ended to serve my own means. Even if I did not do so intentionally so that he could be killed, if I was omniscient (like the Christian God), then I would know he would be put to death anyway. In either instance, intentional or not, this kind of behavior is morally reprehensible. Believing such a God is all loving and deserving of worship is irrational. Basing a religion around such a being is nonsense.[2]

This kind of incessant rhetoric takes a toll on professed believers. It tends to intimidate professed believers to compromise the more offensive elements of the cross and tailor both their message and methods to standards that are more acceptable to social moods.

In what way does the irreverence of the world affect professed believers? It wears on our courage and commitment to Biblical integrity.

The desire to soft-peddle the more offensive aspects of the gospel and to remake the image of Christianity in less confrontational terms is the impetus behind popular marketing strategies in the "Church Growth Movement."

This quest to make churches more "user-friendly" and to remove the potential hurdles to unbelievers has led to an entirely new vocabulary ('churches' are now 'worship' or 'family centers', the 'Holy Bible' is now 'the Message', etc.), a new architecture (pulpit replaced by a stage, traditional sanctuaries by all-purpose rooms, etc.), a new hymnody (feeling-oriented praise choruses instead of theologically-rich traditional hymns), a new homiletic (the sermon is supposed to be 'less preachy, more conversational and entertaining'), and even an attempt to cultivate a new atmosphere for worshippers. It is not uncommon today to see advertisements touting a "relaxed, casual atmosphere" as the dominant feature of a particular group.

Can you imagine Moses coming down from the top of Mt. Sinai with the report that he had just enjoyed a very non-threatening visit with God for forty days in a relaxed, casual atmosphere? This pervasive emphasis on the need to cultivate a "kinder and gentler" Christian testimony has also led to significant controversy among those who want a more contemporary focus in worship and those who favor a traditional emphasis.

Is the controversy over worship styles merely a matter of personal preference? No doubt, in some cases, it is. But I maintain that at the heart and soul of this issue is a philosophical reaction against what is perceived as an oppressive, rigid, and harsh picture of the Christian faith.

Many modern Christians simply do not want a God that is to be feared, but One against whom they can snuggle. They think that the fear of the Lord is an attitude that belongs to the foreboding shadows of the Old Testament, but since the revelation of God's love and grace in Christ, such an attitude has been replaced by an attitude of intimacy, warmth, and freedom. And that leads to the next explanation for this modern aversion to the attitude that the Bible describes as "the fear of the Lord".

Misconceptions Concerning the Nature of This Fear

Thirdly, believers today are uncomfortable with this concept because they tend to confuse the fear of God with the kind of fear that a slave has toward a brutal master.

When the Bible commands us to fear God, it is not talking about the kind of fear experienced by a little boy who cringes at the sight of the neighborhood bully, but the kind of reverential awe and respect that the same little boy exhibits toward the authority of His own loving father. It is the difference between slavish fear and filial submission.

Why did the wicked and slothful servant hide his talent? He was afraid: "...for I feared thee." Why was he afraid? Because he viewed his lord as "a hard" (Mt. 25:24) and "austere man" (Lk. 19:21). His fear of making a mistake paralyzed him from acting. But the kind of fear that makes a person afraid to breathe is not what the Bible means when it commands us to fear God. Godly fear neither leads to paralysis or to panic, but to obedience and confidence.

Other professed believers resist this concept because they mistake godly fear for unbelief. They cannot conceive how a person can both fear God and trust God at the same time. As far as they are concerned, fear is the antithesis of faith. But when Noah constructed the ark, he acted in both faith and fear: *"By faith Noah, being warned of God of things not seen as yet, moved with fear, prepared an ark to the saving of his house..."* (Heb. 11:7).

Godly fear is not the opposite of faith in God. It is faith's corollary, for "in the fear of the Lord is strong confidence" (Pro. 14:26).

Perhaps to the majority of Christian people, the fear of the Lord seems inconsistent with the love of God. "I thought the Bible says," someone responds, 'perfect love casts out fear' (1 Jno. 4:18). How can a person fear God and love God simultaneously? God is love and we should never be afraid of a loving God."

But again, it is important to note that Biblical "love" is not synonymous with "sentimentality." God's love does not mean that He is indulgent and tolerant of evil. Instead, He loves His children enough to discipline them: "As many as I love, I rebuke and chasten; be zealous therefore and repent" (Rev. 3:19).

Our loving Father in heaven is a "Holy Father" and a "Righteous Father" (Jno. 17:11, 25), in whose sight sin is reprehensible. A child's knowledge that he is genuinely loved by his father does not breed contempt and disrespect, but reverential awe, a desire to please him by obedience to his laws, and a dread of displeasing such a good and kind father.

Indeed, "perfect love casts out" the fear of man (Pro. 29:25). And "perfect love casts out" the fear of death (Heb. 2:16). And "perfect love casts out" the slavish fear and dread of punishment (1 Jno. 4:17). But "perfect love" is not inconsistent with an attitude of reverential respect for the heavenly Father.

Rediscovering Reverence

The very fact that this theme sounds strange and foreign to many who believe in Christ today is evidence that we have lost an emphasis that is basic and fundamental to Christianity. Modern man is far too casual and cavalier in his approach to God. The sense of awe and wonder so typical of authentic worship is conspicuous by its absence today.

Why have we suffered this tragic loss? Principally, because we have lost sight of the majesty, holiness, and sovereignty of God. A. W. Tozer hits the proverbial nail on the head:

The church has surrendered her once lofty concept of God...With our loss of the sense of majesty has come the further loss of religious awe and consciousness of the divine presence. We have lost our spirit of worship and our ability to withdraw inwardly to meet God in adoring silence...Always the most revealing thing about the church is her idea of God...The essence of idolatry is the entertainment of thoughts about God that are unworthy of Him. The heaviest obligation lying upon the Christian church today is to purify and elevate her concept of God until it is once more worthy of Him.[3]

The great need of the hour is the recovery of a Biblical understanding of the character of God. That will lead necessarily to a corresponding attitude of reverence and godly fear.

In the article referenced earlier, John Franklin tells of a conversation he had with Henry Blackaby. Blackaby was talking about what it would take for a moral and spiritual turnaround in our land, and he noted that every great spiritual awakening rediscovered some lost truth about God. Franklin says, "Unable to contain my curiosity, I asked him, 'What is it in our day?' Without the least hesitation, he replied, 'The fear of God'."[4]

A Portrait of a God-Fearing Person

Solomon said, *"Favor is deceitful and beauty is vain, but a woman who fears the Lord, she shall be praised"* (Pro. 31:30).

In Scripture, the fear of the Lord is the distinctive mark that characterizes the people of God: *"Come and hear, all ye that fear God, and I will declare what he has done for my soul"* (Ps. 66:16); *"Like as a father pitieth his children, so the Lord pitieth them that fear Him"* (Ps. 103:13); *"I am a companion of all them that fear Thee, and of them that keep Thy precepts"* (Ps.

119:63). In fact, every aspect of our service to God must be characterized by "reverence and godly fear" if we would please and honor Him (Heb. 12:28)

When we sketch a composite of the God-fearing man or woman from the word of God, the portrait that emerges is of a person whose external piety is governed by this inward attitude of reverential awe. What are some of the distinguishing traits of a God-fearing person?

♦   He is compassionate toward others (Gen. 42:18). Joseph teaches us that a bitter and unforgiving spirit is inconsistent with the fear of the Lord.
♦   He is truthful and honest (Ex. 18:21). The fear of the Lord promotes integrity in behavior.
♦   He is single-mined in his devotion to God (1 Sam. 12:24). God is a reality in the life of the individual who fears Him.
♦   He has a respect for the house of God (Ps. 5:7). The person who fears the Lord has a sense of propriety for Divine worship and the standards of God's house.
♦   He is submissive to other believers (Eph. 5:21). A sense of awe and reverence before God makes a man humble and congenial in interpersonal relationships.

In the study that follows, we will explore numerous passages from both the Old Testament and the New regarding the priority of fearing God in the Christian life. The preponderance of Biblical evidence indicates that this subject is central, not peripheral, to godly living. In fact, as John Murray said, "The fear of God is the soul of godliness." It is the very heartbeat of a godly life.

---

[1] *Light*, September-October 1999, p.4
[2] *Kentucky Kernel*, Dec. 9, 1999
[3] A. W. Tozer, *The Knowledge of the Holy*
[4] Franklin, p.4

Chapter 1
The Centrality of 'Fearing God' in Scripture

*"Let us have grace whereby we may serve God acceptably with
reverence and godly fear." Hebrews 12:28*

Near the end of his life, A. W. Tozer commented: *"I've
been assessing the church for a long time and the
conclusion to which I've come is basically this: the church today
is politely bored with God. As a preacher, they want me to say or
do something that will attract their attention, because if I only
talk about God, they will be bored."*

Politely bored! It is not that the average Christian is
ready to dismiss God from his faith or life, but he is not
convinced that God is relevant. He would never admit to
being bored with God – no, he's very polite about it – but,
in the final analysis, he's more interested in success, life-
mastery techniques, and self-help programs than the
knowledge of God revealed in Scripture. He is dissatisfied
with "God talk." He thinks to himself, "There has got to be
something more."

Why is modern man bored with God? Because, in
many cases, the god he has come to know is a mere
caricature of the God of the Bible. "My god would never
condemn anyone to eternal judgment" someone says.
Well, in all due respect, the God of the Bible will.

Stripped of His sovereign majesty by the man-centered
emphasis of the past century and a half, the God of Divine
revelation is virtually unrecognizable to many professing
Christians today. In His place is a god who is handcuffed
by man's refusal to cooperate – who has gone as far as he
can go – who wants to forgive if people will just accept
him. Is it any wonder that modern man is politely bored
with a god who craves acceptance from his creatures?

Instead, the God of Holy Scripture is a God that is *"greatly to be feared in the assembly of the saints and to be had in reverence among all them that are about Him"* (Ps. 89:5). He is a God of ineffable holiness and inscrutable majesty: *"Who is like unto Thee, O Lord, among the gods; glorious in holiness, fearful in praises, doing wonders?"* (Ex. 15:11).

The priority of "fearing God" is affirmed in both testaments. There are over one-hundred-fifty direct references to "the fear of the Lord" in the Bible, not to mention the myriad illustrations and examples of this concept. It is one of the central themes of Scripture—a predominant truth in Biblical thought. The fact that the New Testament, as well as the Old, insists on the priority of walking in the fear of the Lord serves to correct the misconception that "godly fear" is an attitude exclusive to the Law.

A Deterrent to Sin

The first occurrence of the phrase in Scripture is Genesis 20:11: *"And Abraham said, Because I thought, Surely the fear of God is not in this place; and they will slay me for my wife's sake."*

Though Abraham was wrong to lie to Abimelech, he was correct to understand that the fear of the Lord is a deterrent to sin and the absence of such an attitude is the fountain of wickedness (cf. Ecc. 8:12-13; Jer. 5:23-24; Mal. 3:5).

When Pharoah decreed that every male child born to the Hebrews be slain at birth, the Egyptian midwives, Shiphrah and Puah, conscientiously revolted against the unjust law. They "did not as the king of Egypt commanded them, but saved the men children alive" for "the midwives feared God" (Ex. 1:17). And "because they feared God," the Lord blessed the midwives and gave them families (1:20-21).

Writing about the relationship between godly fear and sin, John Calvin said, "All wickedness flows from a disregard of God...Since the fear of God is the bridle by which our wickedness is held in check, its removal frees us to indulge in every kind of licentious conduct."

Calvin is correct. Because Amalek "feared not God," he attacked the feeblest of the children of Israel as they marched through the wilderness (Deut. 25:17-18). Had God been a reality in his heart, he would have exercised greater caution to avoid the slaughter of the innocents who are especially cared for by the Lord (Ps. 68:5-6).

God is Called "Our Fear"

The second reference is found in Genesis 31:42. Speaking to Laban, Jacob refers to God as *"the God of Abraham and the Fear of Isaac."* Again, in verse 53, Jacob swears by *"the Fear of his father Isaac."*

Through the prophet Isaiah, God warned his people against worshipping the idols of the Assyrians: *"...neither fear ye their fear, nor be afraid. Sanctify the Lord of hosts himself; and let him be your fear, and let him be your dread"* (Is. 8:12b-13). God alone is worthy of worship, for *"holy and reverend is His name"* (Ps. 111:9).

The Lord Jesus taught the priority of fearing God: *"Fear not them which kill the body, but are not able to kill the soul: but rather fear him which is able to destroy both soul and body in hell"* (Mt. 10:28). William Gurnall, author of the Christian Classic *The Christian in Complete Armor*, said, "We fear men so much because we fear God so little. One fear cures another." Indeed, when a person ceases to fear God, he begins to fear everything else—calamity (Pro. 1:28-29; Ps.

112:7), man's disapproval (Pro. 29:25), and death (Heb. 2:15).

God's Word Teaches Us How to Fear God

Thirdly, Israel was given God's word *"that they may learn to fear me all the days that they shall live upon the earth, and that they may teach their children"* (Deut. 4:9-10). In Psalm 19, David celebrates the sufficiency of God's word (vs. 7-9). Among the phrases employed to describe the attributes of the word of God, he includes the following: *"The fear of the Lord is clean, enduring for ever"* (Ps. 19:9). God's word is called "the fear of the Lord" because it guides and directs a person how to fear God.

A Characteristic of God's People

Next, the Bible teaches that the fear of the Lord is a distinguishing trait of the people of God. Nehemiah referred to God's true servants as those *"who desire to fear Thy name"* (Neh. 1:11). He appointed Hanani ruler over Jerusalem *"for he was a faithful man, and feared God above many"* (Neh. 7:2).

The Psalms frequently describe the people of God by this distinction: *"Come and hear, all ye that fear God, and I will declare what he hath done for my soul"* (Ps. 66:16); *"For as the heaven is high above the earth, so great is his mercy toward them that fear him...Like as a father pitieth his children, so the Lord pitieth them that fear him...But the mercy of the Lord is from everlasting to everlasting upon them that fear him..."* (Ps. 103: 11, 13, 17); *"I am a companion of all them that fear Thee, and of them that keep Thy precepts"* (Ps. 119:63); *"The Lord taketh pleasure in them that fear him, in those that hope in his mercy"* (Ps. 147:11).

Why do they fear God? Because He graciously gives them a heart to fear Him according to His covenant purpose (Jer. 32:38-39).

The book of Malachi employs this phrase as the dominant characteristic of the faithful remnant in an apostate society. Though the people of Israel had largely revolted from God and refused to fear him (Mal. 1:6), there was yet a godly remnant who "feared God's name" (Mal. 2:5; 3:16; 4:2).

Even in the New Testament, this attitude was a dominant characteristic of the early church. Acts 9:31 says, *"Then had the churches rest...and were edified; and walking in the fear of the Lord, and in the comfort of the Holy Ghost, were multiplied."*

A Characteristic of the Lord Jesus Christ

Further, the prophet Isaiah prophesied that the Messiah would be characterized by the fear of the Lord: *"And the spirit of the Lord shall rest upon him...the spirit of knowledge and of the fear of the Lord; and shall make him of quick understanding in the fear of the Lord..."* (Is. 11:2-3). The writer to the Hebrews indicates that his prayers were heard because *"he feared"* (Heb. 5:7). Surely if the character of the Lord Jesus was marked by godly fear, it is an appropriate attitude for all who call themselves His disciples.

The Foundation of Godly Living

The fear of the Lord is also basic to piety and godliness. Job was a God-fearing man (Job 1:1). The soul of his external piety was this inward fear of God. In a statement almost as familiar as the Golden Rule, Solomon says, *"The fear of the Lord is the beginning of wisdom and the knowledge of the Holy is understanding"* (Pro. 9:10). What is the foundation of godly living ["wisdom" in Proverbs is not shrewd judgment but godliness]? What is the bottom line of devout conduct? The fear of the Lord.

No wonder Solomon counseled young people saying, *"Let us hear the conclusion of the whole matter: Fear God and keep his commandments, for this is the whole duty of man"* (Ecc. 12:13). Every aspect of godly living is marked by this attitude:

- **Service to God** – *"Serve the Lord with fear and rejoice with trembling"* (Ps. 2:11); *"Let us...serve God acceptably with reverence and godly fear"* (Heb. 12:28)

- **Worship of God** – *"But as for me, I will come into thy house in the multitude of thy mercy: and in thy fear will I worship toward thy holy temple"* (Ps. 5:7)

- **Goal of Gospel Ministry** – *"God shall bless us; and all the ends of the earth shall fear him"* (Ps. 67:7)

- **Practical Sanctification** – *"Let us cleanse ourselves from all filthiness of the flesh and spirit, perfecting holiness in the fear of God"* (2 Cor. 7:1); *"Work out your own salvation with fear and trembling"* (Phi. 2:12)

- **Interpersonal Relationships** – *"Submitting yourselves one to another in the fear of God"* (Eph. 5:21); *"Servants, obey in all things your masters according to the flesh...in singleness of heart, fearing God"* (Col. 3:22)

- **Daily Walk** – *"And if you call on the Father, who without respect of persons judgeth according to every man's work, pass the time of your sojourning here in fear"* (1 Pet. 1:17)

Without question, the preponderance of Biblical evidence argues for the importance and priority of the fear of God as a distinguishing mark of the people of God, even subsequent to the cross of Christ. May we respond by joining in the song of Moses and the Lamb, saying, *"Great and marvelous are thy works, Lord God Almighty; just and true are thy ways, thou King of saints. Who shall not fear thee, O Lord, and glorify thy name? For thou only art holy..."* (Rev. 15:3-4).

Chapter 2
Beginning to be Wise

The wise man Solomon wrote, *"The fear of the Lord is the beginning of wisdom: and the knowledge of the holy is understanding"* (Pro. 9:10; cf. 1;7; Job 28:28). The quest for wisdom, that is, the desire to be able to understand the world, solve life's problems, make the right decisions, and attain real meaning and purpose in life, begins with an understanding of the character of God.

Begin at the Beginning

Fearing God is the starting line in the race of faith. It is "Wisdom 101," the most basic and fundamental course of study in the quest to be wise. Regardless of academic degrees, socio-economic status, personal sophistication, or intelligence quotient, the individual who does not fear God has not even started to be wise, for "the fear of the Lord is the beginning of wisdom."

The individual who is wise, in other words, is someone who has learned to test every theory, opinion, word of counsel, and idea by the question "Does it start with God or man?" If it doesn't begin with God, it cannot be Divine truth, for wisdom begins with an understanding of the holiness of God.

Modern society is enamored with contrary philosophical voices. How can the Christian sort through the confusion of contradictory ideas and discover what is true? Start by asking these questions:

- Is this theory based on the fact that God exists, that God is real, that God is holy and sovereign, that God is aware of everything that happens and will bring every work to judgment?

- Is it premised upon the foundational truth that God is the ultimate authority to whom man must give an account?

- Does it presuppose that pleasing and glorifying him is the ultimate purpose of man's existence?

If the answer to these questions is "no," then you can be absolutely certain that the idea is secular and false, not Biblical and true. "How," someone asks, "can you make such a dogmatic statement?" I make the statement by virtue of the fact that "the fear of the Lord is the beginning of wisdom."

If a person once learns to ask whether an idea begins with God's glory or man's needs, God's sovereignty or man's rights, God's grace or man's goodness, God's power or man's ability, and God's holiness or man's happiness, he has taken a giant step forward toward the goal of wisdom. This is where a wise and understanding life begins.

Somewhere along the way, in the desire to be practical and to minister compassionately to the hurting, modern believers have slid precariously into a man-centered emphasis that virtually disregards the holiness of God. Pop-christianity is preoccupied today with felt needs, success, life mastery, self-esteem, and positive thinking.

Can you imagine the apostle Paul giving a message on "Learning to Love Yourself in Six Easy Steps?" No, Paul's preaching started with the Lord. He did not present the Christian faith as a power that can do things for us and make people happy. He preached a God-centered, objective gospel that called for a practical response of "repentance toward God and faith toward our Lord Jesus Christ."

Subjectivity is the blight on today's Christian landscape. We are so abysmally self-centered and narcissistic. Further, there is a consensus of opposition within the Christian community today against anything that is perceived as negative, especially references to sin, judgment, eternal punishment, and the wrath of God. The god of modern religion is a bumper-sticker deity who commands little respect, a pious cliché that few take seriously, an illuminated marquee with a cute or humorous turn of the phrase to give passing motorists a momentary chuckle, a clever 'tweet' in one hundred forty characters or less.

Such a low view of God and a kinder, gentler approach to the subject of sin is responsible for the burgeoning attention to subjects like "bitterness against God," "disappointment with God," and "forgiving God" in today's Christian culture. In fact, the mere comfort and ease with which professed believers discuss subjects like this today, thoughts with which Christians of an earlier generation would have been tremendously uncomfortable, is a sad barometer of the theological declension of our day.

In contrast to this modern allergy and aversion to "negative" preaching, the late D. Martyn Lloyd-Jones, in a sermon entitled "The Tragedy of Modern Man," traced declining church attendance, not to the excessive emphasis of, but the neglect and loss of a Biblical view of God's holiness:

> It is as the idea of judgment and the wrath of God have fallen into the background that our churches have become increasingly empty. The idea has gained currency that the love of God somehow covers everything, and that it matters very little what we may do, because the love of

God will put everything right at the end. The more the Church has accommodated her message to suit the palate of the people the greater has been the decline in attendance at places of worship.

The need of the hour, according to Lloyd-Jones, is the rediscovery of the tragic view of man in sin that is taught in the Bible, not more of the complacent, optimistic view of man that has dominated Christian thinking for so long. Wisdom, i.e. thinking like God thinks about life and the world, begins with an understanding of and reverent response to the holy character of God.

Although the fear of God is not the only attitude that people should have toward the Lord, it is, nonetheless, basic and fundamental to righteousness. Man cannot trifle with God. Serving him is serious business. The individual who has come thus far has begun a journey on the path that leads to godly wisdom.

ABC's and 123's

There is still a further thought in Proverbs 9:10. The word 'beginning" conveys the idea of "the chief part": *"The fear of the Lord is the chief part of wisdom."*

This attitude is the very foundation—the heart and soul—of godliness. Let me illustrate.

A little child goes to kindergarten and learns the alphabet—"A, B, C, D, E, F, G..." He also learns his numbers—"1, 2, 3...8, 9, 10." These simple characters and concepts form the very foundation of everything else he will ever learn in school.

Though he will, in fact, graduate beyond singing the "ABC" song and counting to ten, yet every literary exercise and every algebraic and trigonometric function will be based on these basic concepts. They are the building blocks to education.

In the same way, the Christian may indeed grow in his love for and trust in God, but he will never completely disconnect himself from this foundation of reverence for God.

When Solomon says, therefore, that "the fear of the Lord is the beginning of wisdom," he means that the person who thinks in terms of God's existence and personal presence in the world will be preeminently concerned with pleasing God by taking Him at His word regarding every facet of his thinking and living.

A wise person is someone who has adopted God's view of life and the world. He thinks God's thoughts after Him. He looks at life through the grid of God's word, the Bible, and comes to the same conclusions as Scripture.

Consider, for instance, a child who accepts the testimony of Genesis 1 concerning the origin of the universe, yet who must sit in the classroom of an educator who embraces Darwinian evolution.

Which person has the greater IQ—the student or the professor? Obviously, the teacher is intellectually superior. But who possesses the most wisdom? The child is wiser, because his worldview is rooted in the knowledge of the Creator God.

Perhaps David had just such an example in mind when he wrote, *"I have more understanding than all my teachers: for thy testimonies are my meditation"* (Ps. 119:99). Indeed, the fear of the Lord is the beginning of wisdom.

Learning to Fear God

Why, then, does one person fear God and another doesn't? God's word teaches that a spirit of godly fear is a gift of Divine grace.

Man does not by nature fear the Lord (Rom. 3:18). Unless he experiences a radical change of heart in regeneration (Ps. 55:19), the natural man will say with Pharoah, 'Who is the Lord that I should obey His voice?" (Ex. 5:2). At the most basic level, only God can teach someone to fear Him.

"Tis Grace that taught my heart to fear, and grace my fears relieved."

So, godly fear is an evidence of a gracious state (Acts 10:35; Lk. 23:40). The natural man is not a God-fearer. Show me a God-fearing person and I will show you someone who gives evidence of a work of grace in his heart (Acts 10:2; Rom. 3:18).

When the penitent thief asked his fellow malefactor, "Dost thou not fear God, seeing we are in the same condemnation?" (Lk. 23:40), the other might have sincerely replied, "Look who's talking! I haven't said anything about Jesus that you haven't also said," and he would have been correct. Matthew's account of this scene indicates that at one point, both thieves reviled and reproached Jesus (Mt. 27:44). But somewhere between Matthew 27:44 and Luke 23:40, the Holy Spirit quickened the one thief from spiritual death to spiritual life (Eph. 2:1-4).

How do I know that the thief on the cross was radically transformed by divine grace while he was suspended on crossbeams? His change of heart is now evident by the presence of this attitude of godly fear. In fact, the man who previously joined in ridiculing Jesus is now aghast that his impious fellow could speak so disrespectfully toward the innocent and impeccable Lamb of God.

The natural man, again, does not fear God. Where such godly fear is present, it testifies to the fact that the heart has been touched and tendered by the sovereign work of the Holy Spirit. And it is to those who have already been taught by the Lord to fear Him that the gospel is sent: "Men and brethren, children of the stock of Abraham, and whosoever among you feareth God, to you is the word of this salvation sent" (Acts 13:26).

Those who have been taught of God to fear Him, however, must be further taught *how to* fear Him. A man may not be a stranger to this subject in his experience—i.e. he has the fear of God in his heart—but he may very well be a stranger to it in his daily walk and conduct.

What must a child of God learn about fearing the Lord? The born-again child of God needs to be instructed what it means to fear the Lord—*"Come, ye children, hearken to me, and I will **teach you the fear of the Lord**"* (Ps. 34:11). Further, he needs to be exposed to God's word in order to know how to fear Him—*"...and he shall read therein all the days of his life that he may **learn to fear** the Lord his God..."* (Deut. 17:19).

He must learn that to fear the Lord means "to depart from evil" (Job 28:28) and "to do His commandments" (Ps. 111:10). To further instruct the minds of them whose hearts have been taught to fear God, we will proceed in the next few chapters to offer several definitions of this important concept.

Chapter 3
Standing in Awe of God

"Stand in awe, and sin not." Psalm 4:4

People who have an experimental knowledge of the fear of God need also to develop a theoretical knowledge of this concept. What, then, does the Bible mean by the expression "the fear of the Lord"? What is the nature of the grace of fear—this fundamental virtue of the covenant of grace?

Already, we have made a distinction between *carnal* and *godly* fear. Carnal fear is the kind of anxiety that a child would experience in the presence of the neighborhood bully. Godly fear is the kind of awe and veneration that same child would feel in the presence of the President of the United States.

The fear of God is not that servile fear that views God as a stern taskmaster who can never be pleased. It is rather a filial fear, like a child possesses for the authority of a loving parent. Though the child does not doubt his father's love, yet he understands the principle of submission to the father's authority and dreads to displease him.

John Gill defines the phrase in these filial terms as *"a reverential affection for Him...a fear of offending so good a Being as He."* Indeed, godly fear and sincere love are not antagonists. An old hymn from *Gadsby's Collection* expresses the thought well:

> Fear is a grace which ever dwells
> With its fair partner, love;
> Blending their beauties, both proclaim
> Their source is from above.
> Let terrors fright th'unwilling slave,

The child with joy appears;
Cheerful he does his Father's will,
And loves as much as fears.
Let fear and love, most holy God,
Possess this soul of mine;
Then shall I worship Thee aright,
And taste Thy joys divine.

In specific terms, "the fear of God" is both an attitude —
a settled frame of mind—and an emotion. Rudolph Otto
defined it as *"the emotion of a creature, submerged and
overwhelmed by its own nothingness in contrast to the One who
is supreme above all creatures."*

William Bates said, *"The fear of God is that sanctifying
grace whereby the soul does solemnly and reverently reflect on
God's perfections and from that is moved in all things that
promote God's honor. The love of God is that which constrains
us **to** service; the fear of God is that which checks and restrains
us **from** sin."*

Don Kistler, a contemporary Bible teacher, defines the
concept in these terms: *"The fear of God is that disposition of
heart that sees the smile of God as our greatest reward and the
frown of God as our greatest displeasure."* Theologian John
Murray writes, *"The fear of God...consists in awe, reverence,
honor, and worship...It is the reflex in our consciousness of the
transcendent majesty and holiness of God."*

Sinclair Ferguson, an evangelical pastor and Bible
teacher, describes it as *"that indefinable mixture of reverence,
fear, pleasure, joy and awe which fills our hearts when we realize
who God is and what He has done for us."*

I would define the expression in these terms: *"The fear
of the Lord is a holy caution to avoid sin and a humble
carefulness lest we offend such a holy and gracious God."*

Perhaps the most popular definition is the one that frames this concept in terms of "reverential awe." In the final analysis, I think we can say that the phrase "the fear of the Lord" describes *the emotional response of a person when faced with the reality of the infinite holiness and glory of God, issuing in a mindset of awe and reverence toward Him.*

Our God is an Awesome God

Such a sense of reverential awe is captured in the Holy Spirit's imperative of Psalm 4:4: *"Stand in awe and sin not: commune with your own heart upon your bed, and be still. Selah."*

The Hebrew word translated by the phrase "stand in awe" is *zgr* (pronounced *ragaz*). It means "to tremble, either in anger or fear." Interestingly, Paul quotes this verse in Ephesians 4:26 and applies it to the subject of controlling righteous anger by dealing with it before day's end.

The word also describes a trembling that arises from a sense of intimidation, leading to a holy caution to avoid sin: "Stand in awe and sin not."

In Psalm 33:8-9, David summons the entire creation to reverential awe of the Creator: *"Let all the earth fear the Lord: let all the inhabitants of the world stand in awe of Him. For He spake, and it was done; He commanded, and it stood fast."* What is more awe-inspiring than a Being that creates reality by merely speaking?

In Psalm 119:161, the Psalmist confesses that this spirit of reverential awe toward God translates into a spirit of trembling before His word: *"Princes have persecuted me without a cause: but my heart standeth in awe of Thy word."*

People are called to "stand in awe" of God simply because of who He is. The God of the Bible is uniquely

qualified to be feared (Ex. 15:13; Ecc. 3:14), for He is the
"living God" (Dan. 6:26-27). Jeremiah expresses holy
wonder that anyone would not fear this exclusively great
God: *"Who would not fear Thee, O King of nations?...there is
none like unto Thee"* (Jer. 10:6-7).

Holy Scripture frequently speaks of God as One who is
"terrible," a synonym for "awesome" (Neh. 1:5; 4:14; 9:32).
His name is terrible (Ps. 99:3). So are His works (Ps. 66:3;
106:22; 145:3; Is. 64:3), and His judgments (Joel 2:11; Zeph.
2:11). He alone is to be worshiped, "for the Lord most high
is terrible; He is a great King over all the earth" (Ps. 47:2).

What is "awe"? The Oxford English Dictionary defines
"awe" as "dread mingled with veneration, as of the Divine
Being; solemn and reverential wonder, tinged with latent
fear, inspired by what is sublime and majestic in nature."

Notice the assortment of emotions expressed in the
definition:

- *dread*　(or apprehension)
- *veneration* (or respect)
- *wonder* (or admiration), and
- *fear* (or caution)

When the Bible speaks of "the fear of the Lord", it is
precisely a composite picture of these various emotions
that is under consideration.

God is More Awesome Than His Creation

Let me illustrate the paradox of how this spirit of
wonder is mingled with a sense of healthy respect and
even caution for something majestic.

On a family outing several years ago, we hiked a nature
trail in the mountains.　On the path was a "scenic

overlook" that was simply breathtaking. We were literally awestruck as we peered over the railing, down the steep ledge to the beautiful scene below.

But as a father, my sense of amazement and wonder was mitigated by an acute awareness that we were standing in a potentially dangerous situation. As the children moved increasingly closer to the edge, I sensed that they could easily lose balance, slip through the railing, and fall to their death. The awe I felt at the majesty of the landscape was mixed with a healthy respect for potential hazards.

I have experienced similar sensations when visiting the zoo. I am inexplicably intrigued by wild animals. Like a little child, I experience a strange sense of wonder and fascination every time I see the lions, the tigers, and the bears. At the same time, I inevitably sense a kind of hesitancy and caution at each exhibit. Though several sets of iron bars separate me from these powerful animals, I still feel a need to maintain a respectful distance.

As awe-inspiring as the natural creation is, a view of the God who created it is more awe-inspiring still. Our God is truly an awesome God. The awesome power of tornadoes, hurricanes, earthquakes, and volcanic eruptions are no match for the God who rules the storms: *"The Lord on high is mightier than the noise of many waters, yea, than the mighty waves of the sea"* (Ps. 93:4).

Sigmund Freud posited a psychological explanation for belief in God. He said that mankind invented the idea of God because people are afraid of nature. To help them cope with their phobia of natural catastrophe, they imagined a God who could save them from destruction.

But Luke 8:22-25 refutes Freud's premise. The disciples of Jesus, though afraid of the power of the storm, learned that there is something (or Someone) even more powerful than the forces of nature. Their fear on the Sea of Galilee was quickly replaced by a fear of the One who could command even the winds and the waves to obey Him: *"And they being afraid wondered, saying one to another, What manner of man is this!"*

If a view of the Grand Canyon or Niagara Falls strikes us with an overwhelming sense of wonder and awe, should we not stand in greater awe of the majestic God who created these things? If the size and power of the ocean intimidates us, should we not stand in greater awe at the One who "measures the waters in the hollow of his hand" (Is. 40:12)? Such is the "reverential" awe David must have felt as he gazed upon the starry heavens (Ps. 8:2).

Scripture attests that nature itself trembles and quakes before the God who created it. Job 26:11 says that the *"pillars of heaven tremble and are astonished at His reproof."*

When Isaiah saw the King seated upon His sovereign throne and heard the seraphim cry in antiphonal song, "Holy, holy, holy is the Lord of hosts," the threshold of the house trembled (Is. 6:4).

When God descended on Sinai, the mountain trembled and shook (Ex. 19:18). In fact, *"so terrible was the sight that Moses said, I exceedingly fear and quake"* (Heb. 12:21). Even demons tremble before Him (Jas. 2:19).

In a vivid poetic expression of the Exodus, David describes the earth shaking and quaking at the blast of His nostrils (Ps. 18:7-16). Before such a great God, the only proper response is to stand in awe at the God who rules all nature.

God is More Awesome Than Angels

Just as God is more majestic and powerful than nature, so He is more glorious and awesome than angels.

How would you respond if you saw an angel? What sensation do you think the sudden appearance of an angel would produce in your heart? I'm sure that such an experience would be intimidating, to say the least.

Every account in Scripture in which someone encountered an angel indicates that the individual was struck with fear. In contrast to artistic representations of angels as little chubby babies with wings, the vision of a real angel is evidently a startling and intimidating sight. In virtually every Biblical reference, the angel felt it necessary to introduce his message with the words, "Fear not" (Judges 13:6, 20-23; Dan. 10:18-19; Lk. 1:11-13, 26-30).

If an encounter with an angel is such a staggering and impressive experience, what must it be to encounter the God who commands these heavenly creatures? Even the angels bow in reverential awe before Him.

Awestruck by the Presence of God

In his *Institutes of the Christian Religion,* John Calvin speaks of "that dread and wonder with which Scripture commonly represents the saints as stricken and overcome whenever they felt the presence of God."

When Jacob awoke from his dream at Bethel, he exclaimed, *"Surely the Lord is in this place; and I knew it not...How dreadful is this place! This is none other but the house of God, and this is the gate of heaven"* (Gen. 28:16-17). Later, on his way to meet his brother Esau, Jacob struggled with a feeling of dread of the coming confrontation. That night, the angel of the Lord appeared to him and wrestled with him until daybreak. Can you imagine anything more disconcerting? The next morning, he named the place Peniel, for he said, "*I have seen God face to face, and my life is preserved*" (Gen. 32:22-32; cf. Hos. 12:3). After this frightening encounter with God, Jacob no longer was afraid of his brother Esau.

Likewise, Job was struck dumb by a revelation of God. When Job's desire to reason with the Almighty was finally granted, he could not open his mouth. He was rushed off his feet by a series of rapid-fire, staccato questions that had the effect of thoroughly intimidating him to silence. He said, "*I have heard of thee by the hearing of the ear, but now mine eye seeth thee; wherefore, I abhor myself and repent in dust and ashes*" (Job 42:5-6).

Similarly, Isaiah's vision of the holiness of God produced a corresponding sense of his own sinfulness and depravity: "*Woe is me, for I am undone, for I am a man of unclean lips and I dwell in the midst of a people of unclean lips; for mine eyes have seen the King, the Lord of hosts*" (Is. 6:1-5).

Over and again, encounters with God are described in traumatic terms. When Ezekiel saw the throne of God and the "appearance of a man above upon it", he "fell upon his face" (Eze. 1:25-28). Likewise, Daniel's vision of the "man clothed in linen" dramatically affected him: "*There remained no strength in me: for my comeliness was turned in me into corruption, and I retained no strength*" (Dan. 10:8-12). Habakkuk's experience was similar: "*O Lord, I have heard thy speech and was afraid...When I heard, my belly trembled; my lips quivered at the voice: rottenness entered into my bones, and I trembled in myself...*" (Hab. 3:2, 16).

Even "that disciple whom Jesus loved," the Apostle John, was overwhelmed by his up-close-and-personal encounter with the Lord. When John saw the risen and glorified Christ, he did not engage him in conversation with chatty familiarity, but "fell at His feet as dead" (Rev. 1:17-18). Every genuine encounter with God is marked by this same reaction of reverential awe.

Such an attitude of awe-filled reverence is the essence of the concept Scripture calls "the fear of the Lord." May we stand in awe, then, before the inscrutable majesty of God. Tremble before His word. Gaze upon Him with holy wonder, yet with the caution of the seraphim who with two wings cover their faces lest they presume to peer into mysteries too glorious and pure for them, for the Lord God is high and lifted up.

Chapter 4
Taking God Seriously

A Biblical analysis of this concept indicates a further definition. The sense of reverential awe toward God that Scripture calls "the fear of the Lord" manifests itself in an attitude that takes Him seriously. God is real in the perceptions of the man who fears Him.

How crucial it is to recover an awareness that God means business in this day of appalling superficiality! The kind of bright and breezy approach to contemporary worship that values laughter above learning and brevity above substance is foreign to the spirit and teaching of the New Testament.

Writing about the deep seriousness of a London church pastored by D. Martyn Lloyd-Jones, the biographer comments on *"the silence which prevailed in the large congregation. The stillness generally deepened as the service proceeded...Regular worshippers at Westminster Chapel had no problem in explaining this stillness...In the words of [a] student from Jamaica, 'It was as if I lost all count of time and space. The eternal truth that I hungered for so deeply was being revealed, and I was caught up body, mind and spirit in the sublime experience of receiving, finding, understanding, knowing...What I experienced was the power of the Word'."*[1]

Of course, this kind of reverent atmosphere cannot be manufactured by force without sliding precariously into legalism. But where deep convictions regarding the holiness of God and authority of His word prevail, the result will be a profoundly sobering and enriching experience of public worship.

Paul's regular use of the *sophron* root (translated "sober") in the pastoral epistles indicates that this attitude of seriousness should mark the believer's entire life, not simply his public worship. Ministers are to be sober—or serious-minded—not frivolous (1 Tim. 3:2; Titus 1:8). So are Christian women (1 Tim. 2:9), children (1 Tim. 2:15), aged men (Titus 2:2), and young men (Titus 2:6). In fact, grace teaches us that all of life is to be lived "soberly" (Titus 2:12).

There are basically three areas in which a deep seriousness should mark the life of the believer. God would have His people serious about *His Word*, about *Sin*, and about *His Chastening Rod*.

Taking His Word Seriously

First, the person who fears God should take His word seriously. He will not lightly dismiss the word of God, turn a deaf ear to it, or attempt to alter it, but will tremble and meekly receive it as the word of the living God (Is. 66:2,5; Ezra 9:4; 10:3; Jas. 1:21; 1 Ths. 2:13).

Godly King Josiah's response to God's word illustrates the seriousness with which a person should approach the word of God. The Lord said to him, "Because thine heart was tender, and thou didst humble thyself before God, when thou heardest his words against this place, and against the inhabitants thereof, and humblest thyself before me, and didst rend thy clothes, and weep before me; I have even heard thee also, saith the Lord" (2 Chr. 34:27).

Exodus 9:13-25 records the plague of hail upon the land of Egypt. In the description of that terrifying judgment that fell, the Holy Spirit tells us that some of Pharoah's servants had learned to take God's word seriously: *"He that feared the word of the Lord among the servants of Pharoah made his servants and his cattle flee into the houses: and he that regarded not the word of the Lord left his servants and his cattle in the field"* (vs. 20-21). To "fear God's word" then, is equivalent to "regarding" or taking seriously His word.

The individual who takes seriously the word of God does not approach the word with a "take-it-or-leave-it" attitude. He does not pick and choose what to affirm and what to deny—whether the narrative of special creation in Genesis 1, the supernatural references to miracles, the uncomfortable declaration of the depths of human depravity, or the frightening prospect of Divine wrath against sin and sinners—but acquiesces to the authority of the whole Bible.

John Bunyan insists that men should fear the word of the Lord because of its Author, for "the word of a king is as the roaring of a lion; where the word of a king is, there is power" (Ecc. 8:14).

The absence of this spirit of godly fear expresses itself by an attitude that "mocks the messengers of God, despises His words, and misuses His prophets" (2 Chr. 36:16).[2] The words of Solomon are sobering: "Whoso despiseth the word shall be destroyed: but he that feareth the commandment shall be rewarded" (Pro. 13:13).

The catalyst of the original sin was Satan's daring assault on the integrity of the word of God (Gen. 3:1). Since that day in the Garden of Eden, he has continued his sinister effort to change God's word. But God gives three warnings against an impudent treatment of His word— one at the beginning, one in the middle, and one at the end of the Bible (Deut. 4:2; Pro. 30:6; Rev. 22:18-19).

The message is clear. The Lord doesn't take kindly to the pride of human critique and maverick innovation. In fact, God has always dealt severely with religious daredevils who presumed to edit His revealed will.

Consider the case of Nadab and Abihu in Leviticus 10. When these two sons of Aaron presumed to innovate the prescribed order of Divine worship by offering "strange fire" upon the altar, God struck them dead on the spot. When Aaron complained at the severity of the judgment, Moses replied, "This is that the Lord spake, saying, I will be sanctified in them that come nigh unto me, and before all the people I will be glorified. And Aaron held his peace" (Lev. 10:4).

In his 400-plus pages on this text, the godly pastor Jeremiah Burroughs comments, "Though the lives of men are dear and precious to God, yet they are not so precious as His glory...if we knew what the glory of God meant, we would not think it so much that the lives of so many men should go for the glory of God. It is mercy that our lives have not gone many times for God's glory."[3]

Consider also the case of Uzzah (1 Chr. 13:7-11). Uzzah, a Kohathite, was responsible for bringing the ark of the covenant back to Jerusalem. When the oxen stumbled, Uzzah reached up his hand to steady the ark, and God smote him dead on the spot.

"You mean to tell me," someone objects, "that God struck Uzzah dead for simply touching the ark? He was only trying to help. He just didn't want it to fall to the ground"

Well, what appears on the surface to be an extreme reaction of excessive severity is really a case of perfect justice. You see, the Kohathites had been explicitly commanded not to "touch" any of the holy things (Num. 4:15). God had commissioned Moses to put rings, or hoops, on the sides of the ark and to fashion sticks for the purpose of inserting into the rings so that the ark might be borne upon the shoulders of the sons of Kohath. The very fact that they were now transporting the ark on this new cart, instead of the way God had prescribed, speaks of compromise. Instead of doing God's work in God's way, they hearkened to someone who daringly ventured, "Hey! I have a better idea."

Because they started on the wrong foot, they soon encountered this circumstance in which the wagon began to tip. Had the sons of Kohath performed the task according to the pattern that God had revealed to Moses, Uzzah would not have been in such a predicament.

No doubt, Uzzah's act was instinctive and spontaneous. But it was not innocent—it was presumptuous. He assumed that the dirt on the ground was less polluted than the sin of his hand. He disregarded God's word in the name of pragmatism.

Taking God's word seriously is a matter of paying attention to Scripture—of taking it personally—of listening to it, conscious that God is speaking to us through it.

This matter of learning to listen more carefully is illustrated by an experience our now twenty-one year old son had when he was only six. Writing about his experience a couple of years later in an essay he titled "The Day I Got Left at Home," he said:

> Wait! Oh no! They left me. One night we had to go to church. My dad told me to go to the van, but I was in the backyard instead. Then I heard the van leave. I ran up the hill. When I got up there they were gone. I felt tears come down my eyes. I started to cry. I thought I would never see them again. I would be alone. I thought bad guys would come and get me. Finally I went to my neighbor's house and asked if they could drive me to my church. They said, "O.K." When we got there my mom was sitting on the bench. At first, I thought she was going to be

mad at me, but when I sat down she hugged me. From now on, I learned to be where my dad tells me to be, and where I am supposed to be.

The Lord knows how to bring His children to the point at which they freely confess, "From now on, I will be where He tells me to be. I will do what He tells me to do. I will take His word seriously."

Taking Sin Seriously

Further, the individual who fears the Lord will take sin seriously. In days of affluence and ease, people tend to excuse sin and fear suffering. Our society laughs at sin and complains against God at suffering. The person who fears the Lord, however, agrees with the old Puritan who said, "Sin is more to be feared than suffering."[4]

God will not allow His people to get away with sin. He is serious about the purity of the church. Consider the case of Ananias and Sapphira recorded in Acts 5:1-11.

Some of the believers in the early church had voluntarily liquidated their assets and contributed the proceeds to the church. Ananias and his wife Sapphira sold a piece of property and pretended to give the entire amount. It was a strictly voluntary act. They were not required either to sell the land or to give the entire amount. When Ananias brought the money to Peter, however, the Lord struck him dead.

Ananias wanted the congregation to know that he, like others before him, was donating the entire proceeds of the sale. But it was a sham. He had kept back a portion of the money for himself. Satan had "filled his heart to lie to the Holy Ghost."

When his wife came into the assembly later, not knowing what had happened to her husband, Peter asked,

"Tell me whether you sold the land for such and such a price?" She replied, "Yes, that was the price." Then Peter said, "How is it that ye have agreed together to tempt the Spirit of the Lord? Behold the feet of them which have buried thy husband are at the door, and shall carry thee out," and she fell dead as well (v. 9).

What was their sin? Were they punished because they refused to sacrifice everything? No. They were judged because they pretended to sacrifice everything while they secretly kept back part of the proceeds. Such dishonesty would set a dangerous precedent in the church and God judged it swiftly and severely. God made these two an example to all who might be tempted to trifle with sin.

What was the effect of this first act of Divine discipline in the church? The result was that *"great fear came upon all the church, and upon as many as heard these things"* (v. 11).

Commenting on the effect that this display of Divine discipline had on the church, one pastor writes: *"You can be certain there was a lot of careful self-examination going on in the Jerusalem church that day. And that was the point. God was purifying His church. He wanted His people to take sin seriously. He wanted to discourage shallow commitment. He wanted the people to fear Him...The issue is not what unbelievers think about such severity; it is what God thinks about such iniquity."*[5]

Taking His Chastening Rod Seriously

An old adage says, "There are times when a person must be perceived as cruel in order to be kind." Though we tend to recoil at the thought, yet it expresses an axiomatic principle for life.

Every doctor knows that he must sometimes cause temporary pain for the long-term welfare of the patient. It is a difficult task for the physician to inject a needle into a deep cut and the patient may think he is being unusually severe, but if the wound is to be stitched for healing, the temporary "cruelty" is actually an expression of kindness, for it aims at the patient's long-term interest.

This principle is the basis for applying the rod of correction in training children. Though it is an unpleasant task from which every parent naturally shrinks, it is something he must do, for "foolishness is bound in the heart of a child, but the rod of correction will drive it far from him" (Pro. 29:15,17; 19:18). Though the child may think the parent especially cruel, discipline is really a proof of love (Pro. 13:24).

The Lord also disciplines His children because He loves them (Pro. 3:12; Rev. 3:19). In fact, the absence of Divine chastening in a person's life is evidence that such a one is not a child of God, for "whom the Lord loveth he chasteneth and scourgeth every son whom He receiveth" (Heb. 12:6-8).

How is Divine chastening a proof of love? Chastening proves that the Father loves his children enough to check and challenge sinful conduct. Divine chastening is the Heavenly Father's child-training program to grow His children toward spiritual maturity: "He [chastens us] for our profit, that we might be partakers of His holiness" (Heb. 12:10).

The chastening rod of God, however, is not pleasant; and no one who has ever experienced it would court such an experience of the Heavenly Father's displeasure. The believer does not doubt God's love—he does not fear eternal punishment (1 Jno. 4:17)—but at the same time, he soon develops a healthy respect for the rod of correction and an understanding that willful defiance will bring remedial and corrective discipline.

Discipline is not intended to be an enjoyable experience, "but grievous"; nevertheless, over time, it "yields the peaceable fruit of righteousness unto them that are exercised thereby" (Heb. 12:11). Notice it is only the individual that heeds the lesson or responds positively to the discipline—i.e. that is "exercised thereby"—who profits from the pain of chastening. When God's child submits to it in meekness and humility (as opposed to either "despising" it or "fainting" at it – v. 5), however, he learns that disobedience brings painful consequences and, little by little, that the best path is submission to His word (Ps. 119:67,71).

At the dedication of the temple, Solomon prayed that God would answer the prayers of His people, "that they may fear thee, to walk in thy ways" (2 Chr. 6:31). The words teach that godly fear expresses itself in obedience to God.

My good friend Elder Joe Holder writes, "Fearing God enough to walk in his ways when the masses around us are walking in another direction and pushing us to get in step is what this lesson is all about."[6] This is the end at which the Heavenly Father aims in Divine chastening. We learn obedience by the things that we suffer. We learn to take God seriously.

> Thy people, Lord, have ever found
> 'Tis good to bear Thy rod;
> Afflictions make us learn Thy will,
> And lean upon our God.
> This is the comfort we enjoy
> When new distress begins;

We read Thy word, we run Thy way,
We hate our former sins.
Thy judgments, Lord, are always right,
Tho' they may seem severe;
The sharpest sufferings we endure,
Flow from Thy faithful care.
Before we knew Thy chastening rod,
Our feet were apt to stray;
But now we learn to keep Thy word,
Nor wander from Thy way.

[1] Iain Murray, *D. M. Lloyd-Jones: The Fight of Faith*, pp. 265-66.
[2] John Bunyan, *The Fear of God*, p. 20.
[3] Jeremiah Burroughs, *Gospel Worship*, p. 34-35.
[4] Burroughs, *The Evil of Evils*, p.
[5] John MacArthur, *Ashamed of the Gospel*, p. 62.
[6] Joseph R. Holder, *Fear*, p. 21.

Chapter 5
A Holy Caution

In Psalm 34:9-18, a further definition of Biblical "fear" emerges. In verses 9-12, David invites others to learn the meaning of *the fear of the Lord*: "Come, ye children, hearken unto me: I will teach you the fear of the Lord..." (v. 11).

Then, in verses 13-14, David defines "fearing God" in terms of *a holy caution to avoid sin and a humble carefulness lest we offend the Lord*: "Keep thy tongue from evil, and thy lips from speaking guile. Depart from evil, and do good; seek peace, and pursue it."

This kind of holy caution is the essence of godly fear. The truly wise person is someone that, because he fears God, does not live with reckless abandon, like the proverbial bull in a china shop. He doesn't rush in foolishly where angels fear to tread. If the mysterious seraphim who dwell in God's presence employ four of their six wings in the act of covering their faces and feet (Is. 6:1ff), why would sinful mortals live carelessly and heedlessly before Him.

Instead, the wise man, like Hezekiah of old, "goes softly all his years" (Is. 38:15), carefully tiptoeing through the precarious minefield of life, lest he fall into temptation and sin. He "walks circumspectly [lit. carefully and accurately], redeeming the time because the days are evil" (Eph. 5:15). Notice the suggested thought of "caution" in these references.

Ecclesiastes 5:1-7 presents a graphic description of "holy caution":

Keep thy foot when thou goest to the house of God, and be more ready to hear, than to give the sacrifice of fools: for they consider not that they do evil. Be not rash with thy mouth and let not thine heart be hasty to utter any thing before God: for God is in heaven, and thou upon earth: therefore let thy words be few...When thou vowest a vow unto God, defer not to pay it...Suffer not thy mouth to cause thy flesh to sin...but fear thou God.

The "Preacher" encourages his young auditors to exercise an attitude of caution or hesitancy before God in the area of their daily walk ("keep thy foot"), their words, and their vows (or promises).

Many people live carelessly, without consideration of how their words or deeds will affect others. Even rarer is the person who considers the Lord when it comes to judging the appropriateness of behavior: "they consider not that they do evil" (Ecc. 5:1b). Perhaps it would be well if many older Christians learned to sing the little child's song again:

> Be careful little lips what you say...
> Be careful little eyes what you see...
> Be careful little ears what you hear...
> Be careful little feet where you go...
> For the Lord is up above,
> He is looking down in love,
> So be careful little lips what you say.

The person who fears God knows that sin hides God's face from him (Is. 59:2), and that unconfessed sin eventually provokes the Lord to abandon the impenitent sinner to the consequences of his own behavior (Rom. 1:24-28; 1 Jno. 5:16). Further, he is aware that when God withdraws his blessing, favor, and providential intervention in the affairs of daily life, people tend to self-destruct.

How quickly life falls apart when the Lord, in his righteous displeasure, removes his restraining influence from our lives! What utter folly it is to offend our gracious God!

Arises from a Sense of Personal Weakness

Why does the Christian live with an attitude of caution and carefulness? First, because he is conscious of his own weakness. He knows that he is *"prone to wander...prone to leave the God [he] loves."* Experience has taught him his own tendency to stumble and he has learned to distrust himself.

The language of 2 Corinthians 7:11 expresses this point in terms of the many emotions that are generated in a repentant heart: *"Ye sorrowed after a godly sort, what carefulness it wrought in you, yea, what clearing of yourselves, yea, what indignation, yea, what fear, yea, what vehement desire, yea, what zeal, yea, what revenge!"*

The Corinthians had learned a painful lesson. Their godly repentance manifested itself in a dramatic change of behavior. They were no longer "puffed up in pride" at their sophisticated and tolerant attitude (1 Cor. 5:2). The pain of sin had generated a more cautious and reverent attitude in them. They now knew just how easily they could be deceived into disobedience.

This awareness of my potential to stumble and to fall prompts me to sing, *"I am weak, but Thou art strong; Jesus keep me from all wrong."* The hymnwriter, evidently, understood the significance of the last petition in the model prayer: *"Lead us not into temptation, but deliver us from evil"* (Mt. 6:13).

The request in Matthew 6:13 is a parallelism—the second phrase explains the first. Jesus teaches his disciples to pray, in other words, "Lord, keep me from falling, for I know my potential to fall into sin. When I have the inclination, keep me from the opportunity; when I have the opportunity, keep me from the inclination."

This is precisely the mindset that moved Charles Wesley to write:

> I want a principle within of watchful, godly fear,
> A sensibility of sin, a pain to feel it near.
> Help me the first approach to feel of pride or wrong desire;
> To catch the wandering of my will,
> And quench the kindling fire.
> From Thee that I no more may stray,
> No more Thy goodness grieve,
> Grant me the filial awe, I pray, the tender conscience give.
> Quick as the apple of an eye, O God, my conscience make!
> Awake my soul when sin is nigh, and keep it still awake.

The individual who fears the Lord is conscious of the precarious position he is in by virtue of his fallen nature. He has no illusions of grandeur. He hears the warnings of Scripture—the "take heeds" and "bewares"—as God's personal flashing "caution signals" to him (Mt. 18:10; Lk. 12:15; 1 Cor. 3:10; Heb. 2:1; Heb. 3:12; Deut. 6:12; Col. 2:8; 2 Pet. 3:17).

What danger we are in of dishonoring the Lord Jesus Christ and discrediting the ongoing work of his kingdom in the earth! Satan knows that if he can make caricatures of God's people by tempting them to react carnally to the circumstances of life, he has dealt a strategic blow to Christ's kingdom and robbed the Lord of glory. How carefully we must live, lest we displease our Lord and give the devil a foothold against us!

The person who fears God knows his own frailty, weakness, and tendency to wander from the path of godliness. He does not trust himself, but expresses his own helplessness and total dependence on the Lord for strength and grace to be holy.

Arises from Sense of Divine Privilege

Secondly, this attitude of holy caution arises from an awareness of the preciousness of God's blessings. Just as a person who had purchased a valuable work of art would be cautious lest the canvas was marred, so the believer who understands the value of Divine grace will exercise care and caution lest he risk the loss of these blessings.

Romans 11:20-21 says, *"Well; because of unbelief they were broken off, and thou standest by faith. Be not highminded, but fear: for if God spared not the natural branches, take heed lest he also spare not thee."*

Paul's argument to these Gentile Christians is clear: *The privileges of the Gospel of Christ call for holy caution, lest we abuse His grace and incur the same judgment suffered by the natural descendents of Abraham.*

The twin command to "quench not" and "grieve not the Holy Spirit" (1 Ths. 5:19; Eph. 4:30) argues from this same principle. Sin in the believer's life shows a lack of concern for and consideration of this Sacred Guest in the soul. When we offend Him, we offend our best Friend, and rob ourselves of the privileges of His sweet influence in our lives.

The fear of the Lord is an automatic warning system in the soul—a flashing caution signal in the renewed conscience that serves to keep the Christian in the will of God. Like Charles Wesley, every believer should pray for *"a principle within of watchful, godly fear; a sensibility to sin, a pain to feel it near."*

Chapter 6
Practicing the Presence of God

Psalm 34:15-16 further defines the "fear of the Lord" in terms of **a conscious awareness that God is watching**: *"The eyes of the Lord are upon the righteous, and his ears are open unto their cry. The face of the Lord is against them that do evil, to cut off the remembrance of them from the earth."*

The individual who fears God lives each moment in conscious awareness of God's presence. He knows that every thought, word, and deed is before the face of God (Gen. 17:1).

David made a deliberate and conscious effort every day to remember that he lived under the scrutiny of the Divine gaze: *"I have set the Lord always before me: because He is at my right hand, I shall not be moved"* (Ps. 16:8). We might say that David disciplined himself to "practice the presence of God."

Elder T. L. Webb, Jr., a godly pastor, illustrates the discipline of practicing the Divine presence in a very practical way. He writes,

> If each time we sit down to discuss anything in the home, in the church, or wherever it might be, we will always place another chair as if someone were sitting there and remind ourselves that our Lord is seated in it, we might be more careful in our conversations and our decisions. Would this not have an effect to remind us of His presence? It seems to take so much to remind us of Him. Let us try always to provide an extra chair.

Learning to live all of life before the face of God is a mark of spiritual maturity. Martin Luther wrote, "To have God always before the eyes makes a lively spirit and an undismayed heart, which is joyful and willing to bear patiently wherever misfortune, the cross, and suffering need to be borne: such a faith is unconquerable."

God Sees and Knows All

The fear of the Lord is the heart's response to the awareness that everything we do is under the scrutiny of the Divine gaze. Scripture unequivocally affirms the omniscience of God. He sees and knows all: *"The Lord is in his holy temple, the Lord's throne is in heaven: his eyes behold, his eyelids try, the children of men"* (Ps. 11:4); *"The eyes of the Lord are in every place, beholding the evil and the good"* (Pro. 15:3; Cf. Job 34:21-22, Ps. 139:1-12, Jer. 23:23-24).

The Lord is always present, whether we are cognizant of Him or not (Acts 17:27; Jon. 1:3). Everything one says, or thinks, or does is done "in His sight." The kings of Israel and Judah are described as doing what was right or what was evil "in his sight" (1 Kings 12:2; 13:2). Paul thanked God for the Thessalonian believers who had demonstrated their faith, love, and hope "in the sight of God our Father" (1 Ths. 1:3). Likewise Peter rebuked Simon the sorcerer because his heart was not right "in the sight of God" (Acts 8:21).

Our God is the "heart-knower" before whose gaze every thought, motive, word, and deed is exposed (Acts 1:24; 15:8; I Sam. 16:9; I Kings 8:39; Ps. 44:21; Jer. 17:10; Rev. 2:23). He is a God who sees, hears, and takes account (Ex. 3:7-8; Mal. 3:16).

Tragically, however, many people live their lives oblivious to the reality of God's presence. For some reason, we seldom stop to think of the reality that "He is not far from every one of us" (Acts 17:27b). People are more real to us than God. We think and say and do things in the full view of God that we would never do if other people were watching. Why? Perhaps the reason is that at a very basic and fundamental level, fallen people like us are more interested in being popular than godly.

Whether or not we are cognizant of the Divine presence, still God is always near. Like Jacob, we need a spiritual awakening that would prompt us to exclaim "The Lord is in this place and I knew it not!" (Gen. 28:16). When a person is suddenly awakened from his spiritual stupor to the awareness that he has been, all along, in the presence of God, albeit oblivious to that fact, he feels the same emotional sensation Jacob expressed at Bethel: "And he was afraid and said, 'How dreadful is this place! This is none other but the house of God, and this is the gate of heaven" (Gen. 28:17).

How blessed are those episodes in personal experience when God has graciously startled you from spiritual slumber, so that like Nebuchadnezzar after his bout of insanity, your "understanding returned unto you" (Dan. 4:34)! Or like the Prodgial, you suddenly came to your senses, startled awake to the contrast between your present misery and the peace that is available to you, and exclaimed, "How many of my father's hired servants have bread enough and to spare, and I perish with hunger!" (Lk. 15:17).

Were it not for these merciful interventions of Providence to rouse us from sleep-walking through life, we would have frittered our lives away in trivial pursuits on an even greater scale than we have already. But once awakened to the reality of God's presence, it is still further necessary to develop the spiritual discipline (or habit) of 'practicing the presence of God.'

In other words, we must cultivate the habit of reminding ourselves every day that He is watching. With David, we must consciously and deliberately "set the Lord always before us."

Notice that such a spiritual discipline did not happen automatically in David's life. It wasn't magic. He says, "I have set the Lord always before me." He did it. He did it consciously. He did it decisively. David made a deliberate and concerted effort each day to remind himself that the Lord was near and that the story of his life that was being played out every day on the stage of human history was being observed very closely by one very important and distinguished Visitor and Friend, the God of heaven.

Before the Face of God

Long before David, Abraham 'practiced the presence of God.' When God told Abram "Walk before me and be thou perfect," he meant that Abram should live every moment with the conscious awareness that God was watching. The phrase "before me" literally means "before my face."

It expresses the thought of living each moment mindful of His presence (Heb. 11:27), submissive to His authority (Rom. 14:6-9), and dedicated to His glory (1 Cor. 10:31).

The basis or foundation of this kind of mindset is the truth that all of life is spiritual (Col. 3:17, 23; Eph. 6:5-6). Contrary to the way most of us live, there are no sacred and secular compartments into which we may categorize our lives. Every dimension of life—domestic, religious, social, political, monetary, vocational, recreational—falls under the canopy of the Lordship of Jesus Christ.

I suspect that many professing Christians are like me. Early on, I developed a template for life that involved living secularly Monday through Saturday, and spiritually for a few hours on Sunday. But no sooner was public worship concluded than I returned to a mindset that was more natural. Then I wondered why the weekdays were invariably marked by relational tension, inner turmoil, rude behavior, and a life that was increasingly chaotic and disorganized.

It wasn't that I disliked the idea of God or was not interested in the church. Instead, I had never even seriously considered the possibility that Monday through Saturday might belong to anyone else but me. Thank the Lord that one day He awakened me from my spiritual daze to realize that I am called to submit to Christ as Lord in every part and parcel of my life, i.e. who I am, where I go, what I do, and how I conduct myself.

When Christ is acknowledged as Lord and "king" in a person's life, the most common details of life are suddenly significant. Even the bells on the horses (i.e. all the trappings—bridles, bits, harnesses, frontlets—on these common animals) and the pots in Jerusalem are "holiness unto the Lord," i.e. dedicated to God as much as the garments of the high priest (Zech. 14:9, 20-21).

Commenting on this intriguing passage in Zechariah 14:20-21, Charles Spurgeon says, "The most common buildings, set apart to meanest uses, being frequented by worshippers of the Lord, shall become temples of Him who dwelleth in humble and contrite hearts." No wonder Brother Lawrence, the cook in a medieval monastery and author of the little classic volume entitled *Practicing the Presence of God*, could worship God in his kitchen amidst the pots and pans, for he saw all of life as an act of worship to God.

The individual who lives his or her life before the face of God desires that Christ have the preeminence in every aspect of his life (Col. 1:18). He acknowledges his complete and utter dependence on the Lord "in all [his] ways" (Pro. 3:5-6). He lives every moment of his life with the aim of pleasing and glorifying God, praying with the Psalmist, *"Let the words of my lips and the meditations of my heart be acceptable in Thy sight, O Lord, my strength and my redeemer"* (Ps. 19:14).

Benefits of Practicing the Divine Presence

What benefit will this practice, or spiritual discipline, have on our lives? First, it will powerfully influence the way we use our words.

Preachers especially need the reminder that God is watching. The knowledge that God sees and hears and takes account will motivate those who speak in His name to integrity. Unlike the majority of religious teachers in his day, Paul could not, in good conscience, twist the Scriptures to a more preferable meaning, for, he says, *"in the sight of God* speak we in Christ" (2 Cor. 2:17). Nothing will be a greater incentive to an accurate interpretation and faithful proclamation of the word of God like the awareness that He is standing beside me in the pulpit, looking over my shoulder.

Also, nothing will be so effective to correct the tendency to sloth and apathy as the awareness that God is here. The Bible does not have a single nice thing to say about laziness. The sluggard is one of the most notorious characters of Solomon's *Proverbs*, with his fields overgrown with weeds and holes in the floor of his house. Solomon had seen plenty of people who perpetually yearned for things to be better in their lives, but couldn't seem to rouse themselves from bed to put forth the effort that is so crucial to every success. He doesn't want his son to indulge that natural tendency to slothfulness, but to live in conscious awareness of the reality of God: *Be not wise in thine own eyes; fear the Lord, and depart from evil. It shall be health to thy navel and marrow to thy bones"* (Pro. 3:7-8).

Further, it will promote godly attitudes in our hearts, such as self-humbling (Jas. 4:10), meekness of spirit (1 Pet. 3:4), and a desire to please Him in everything we do (1 Jno. 3:22). Notice in these verses the repetition of the easily-overlooked phrase *in His sight*: "Humble yourselves *in the sight* of the Lord…"; "…the ornament of a meek and quiet spirit which is *in the sight* of God of great price"; "…then have we confidence toward God and do those things that are pleasing *in his sight.*"

This habit of 'practicing the presence of God' will also foster spiritual stability and consistency in life. That is what David means by the thought "because He is at my right hand I shall not be moved" (Ps. 16:8b).

And it will equip the believer to resist temptation (Gen. 39:9; Cf. Ps. 51:4). In fact, nothing will be a more powerful deterrent to an unholy life than the knowledge that God is present (Acts 4:19). The awareness that "all things are naked and open unto the eyes of him with whom we have to do" is a sobering reminder to those who are prone to sin (Heb. 4:13).

Finally, the awareness that the Lord is present will be one of the most powerful resources to equip the Christian to endure the trials and difficulties of life (Ps. 23:4; Is. 41:10). When the enemy taunts you with the question, "Where is thy God?" you may bid him flee, for Christ is near.

The spiritual instability we see in our lives may almost always be traced to the natural habit of segregating and compartmentalizing life into the duplicitous secular/sacred mindset: "A double-minded man is unstable in all his ways" (Jas. 1:8). The individual who has learned the new, godly, and biblical habit of living consciously before the gaze of God, however, may say with David, "Because He is at my right hand, I shall not be moved."

Chapter 7
Walking Humbly

In addition to these other definitions, fearing God is also closely akin to the attitude that the Bible calls "humility."

Proverbs 3:7 says, "*Be not wise in thine own eyes; fear the Lord, and depart from evil.*" Note the point of contrast in this couplet. According to the wise man, fearing God is antithesis of pride, or the state of being wise in one's own eyes.

Again, Solomon contrasts the attitude of godly fear with pride: "*Happy is the man that feareth always: but he that hardeneth his heart shall fall into mischief*" (Pro. 28:14). If a hardened heart is the opposite of the fear of God, then a tender or humble heart is its counterpart.

Humility (how we see and think of ourselves) is—if you will—one side of the coin of godly attitudes and the fear of the Lord (how we see and think of God) is the other. A person's assessment of himself will always be proportionate to his idea of God. If he has a high view of God—that is, if he fears the Lord—he will have a converse view of his own importance: "*Put them in fear, O Lord; that the nations may know themselves to be but men*" (Ps. 9:20).

It is not possible for man to maintain a high view of God and an inflated opinion of himself simultaneously. Like a pair of old-fashioned balances, as God is exalted in man's esteem, his sense of self-importance is diminished; moreover, when a person has an inflated opinion of himself, his view of God must be lowered proportionately (Jno. 3:30; Ps. 50:21).

Numerous other passages in Scripture join the concepts of humility and the fear of the Lord. Proverbs 15:33 says in a comparative couplet, *"The fear of the Lord is the instruction of wisdom; and before honor is humility."* And Proverbs 22:4 is one of the most striking examples of the relationship that exists between these twin concepts: *"By humility and the fear of the Lord are riches, and honor, and life."*

The Priority of Humility

Fearing God, then, is a matter of "walking humbly with" God every day (Mic. 6:8). An understanding of His character and awareness of His presence will produce a powerful, corresponding impression on a child of God's own self-assessment so that a perpetually humble frame of mind is the result. This is what the Lord requires of us.

Humility is the most basic characteristic of Christian discipleship (Mt. 5:3; Mt. 18:3-4). It is also the goal of God's providential dealings with His children. He employs trials of faith "to humble [them], and to prove [them], and to know what is in [their] heart, whether [they] would keep his commandments or no" (Deut. 8:2). He chastens so that "the spirit should fail before" Him, that is, to break the proud and stubborn will of his rebellious child (Is. 57:16).

Humble people are receptive to the word (2 Chr. 34:27; Jas. 1:21). They do not murmur and complain against the dispensations of Divine providence, but are thankful and content to trust themselves to the God who has already rescued them from eternal ruin (1 Ths. 5:18). They are gentle and agreeable toward others, for they esteem others better than themselves (Eph. 4:2-3; Phi. 2:3-4; Pro. 13:10).

Indeed, God places a high premium on the virtue of humility. Nothing is so reprehensible to him as pride (Pro. 6:16), and nothing so basic and fundamental in importance as the attitude of humility.

Let's sketch a Biblical portrait of the individual who "walks humbly with [his] God".

The Meaning of Humility

What does a humble person look like? First, the humble man is *aware of his sinful condition.*

He readily confesses with the publican, "God be merciful to me a sinner" (Lk. 18:13). He is "poor in spirit" (Mt. 5:3), i.e. a spiritual beggar—a person aware of his bankrupt condition and prepared to admit his own failures. He feels to be the chief of sinners (1 Tim. 1:15)— less than the least of all saints (Eph. 3:8). Because, like Jacob of old (Gen. 32:10), he is so conscious of his own unworthiness, he is ready to confess that God has rewarded him less than his iniquities deserve (Job 11:6; Ezra 9:13; Ps. 103:10). His is not the question of Pharoah— "Who is the Lord that I should obey His voice?"—but the question of Moses—"Who am I?"

Secondly, the humble person is *skeptical of his own ability.* He journeys through life with an acute sense of his own weakness and potential to stumble. The humble man has no illusions of his own ability. Like Paul who came to the Corinthians in "weakness and fear and much trembling" (1 Cor. 2:5), the humble man feels to be inadequate, in and of himself (2 Cor. 3:5). He confesses, "I have nothing, am nothing, and can do nothing apart from Jesus Christ" (Jno. 15:4). He knows that any good thing about him is due to the grace of God (1 Cor. 15:10; ! Cor. 4:7).

Thirdly, the humble man is *sensitive to his own need.* He readily acknowledges with the psalmist, "I am poor and needy" (Ps. 40:17). He possesses an intense awareness of his total dependence on God. He understands the brevity and frailty of his life (Ps. 39:4) and that he knows nothing yet as he ought to know (1 Cor. 8:2).

A true understanding of the character of God will necessarily manifest itself in a humble posture before him: "Talk no more so exceeding proudly; let not arrogancy come out of your mouth: for the Lord is a God of knowledge, and by Him actions are weighed" (1 Sam. 2:3).

When Paul commanded the Philippians to "work out [their] own salvation with fear and trembling" (Phi. 2:12), he did not mean for them to live in perpetual dread that they might not belong to the Lord or that they might lose their salvation. Instead, he meant that they should live their Christian lives with a conscious awareness of their own insignificance, weakness, and fallibility. They must never forget that they were totally dependent on the Spirit of God for Divine enabling. They must never lose sight of own utter helplessness and inability.   Such a humble posture is the attitude that distinguishes authentic faith from sinful self-confidence.

Further, this humble attitude of "fear and trembling" is not merely something that should mark the believer in the earliest stages of his Christian experience. In fact, it should characterize his life as the dominant frame of mind on an ongoing and increasingly intense basis.

It is intriguing to note that Paul's three autobiographical statements in the Epistles reveal an increasing awareness of his own weakness and sinfulness as time passed. In the letter to the Corinthians, written in approximately 56 A.D., he affirmed that he felt to be "the least of the apostles" (1 Cor. 15:9). Later, in the letter to the Ephesians, written in approximately 60 A.D., he admitted that he felt to be "less than the least of all saints" (Eph. 3:8). Then, in his first pastoral epistle to Timothy, written in about 64 A.D., he assumed the title "chief of sinners" (1 Tim. 1:15).

From "least" of the preachers, to "less than the least" of church members, to the worst of "sinners", Paul models the principle that authentic Christian discipleship is characterized by an ever-increasing spirit of humility and self-effacement. Arthur W. Pink put it best: "Growth in grace is like the growth of a cow's tail. The more it grows, the closer it gets to the ground."

This biblical nexus, then, between the fear of the Lord and humility is telling. It means that I am cognizant of the fact that I am dependent on Him for life and breath and all things (Acts 17:25). There is no place for the proud boast of the Laodiceans, "We are rich and increased with goods and have need of nothing" (Rev. 3:14).

Instead, the best place for me is at the feet of Jesus. The God-fearing person gladly assumes such a humble and prostrate posture of reverence, inviting others who fear Him, "O come, let us worship and bow down: let us kneel before the Lord our maker" (Ps. 95:6). And so he passes the brief and uncertain time of his earthly life and pilgrimage in fear (1 Pet. 1:17), walking humbly with his God.

Chapter 8
The Knowledge of the Holy

"The fear of the Lord is the beginning of wisdom: and the knowledge of the holy is understanding." Proverbs 9:10

Having discussed the centrality of godly fear in both testaments and several definitions of this important concept, we move now to a consideration of the source of godly fear. What is the basis of the attitude Scripture calls 'the fear of the Lord'?

Godly fear arises from right views of the character of the God whose name is "Holy and Reverend" (Ps. 111:9). The individual who fears God is a person who thinks great thoughts about God—who sees Him high and lifted up. When our view of God is elevated, our sense of awe and reverence before Him will be increased.

There is something profoundly mysterious and fearful about the nature of God. In his book entitled *The Idea of the Holy*, Rudolph Otto analyzed the paradox of emotions that attend an encounter with God—a concept he called the *mysterium tremendum* or "awful mystery":

> The feeling of it may at times come sweeping like a gentle tide, pervading the mind with a tranquil mood of deepest worship...It may become the hushed, trembling and speechless humility of the creature in the presence of— whom or what? In the presence of that which is a mystery inexpressible and above all creatures.

A consideration of certain Divine attributes—i.e. power, majesty, holiness, justice, wrath, and grace—is especially useful in developing godly fear. These attributes are distinctive of God. They are beyond us—above man's ability to grasp. They remind us of our mortality and frailty; consequently, they frighten us.

In a word, they are "mysterious." People have no point of reference by which to interpret a mystery. Likewise, we have nothing common or familiar by which we can adequately and completely interpret the nature of God. His attributes are foreign and strange to us. They are different from everything with which we are familiar.

His Sovereign Power

One such mysterious and awe-inspiring attribute is His sovereign power. In a matter of a few chapters, Luke records five encounters with the sovereign power of Christ. Each had the effect of highlighting the difference between the Lord Jesus and the people around Him. And each encounter left the audience with a profound and uncomfortable sense of their own inferiority and creaturliness, intensifying the sense that they were in the presence of One they could not completely understand.

First, in Luke 5:1-11, Jesus demonstrated *his sovereign power over creation.* Peter, an experienced fisherman, had toiled all night but caught nothing. At the Lord's instruction to cast the net again, Peter expressed skepticism; after all, Peter was the expert on the scene.

He knew that there were some nights that the best thing to do was pack the gear and go home; nevertheless, he obeyed the Lord Jesus. The catch was so plentiful that the net would not hold the fish, so they signaled to another ship for help. Both ships were so full of fish that they began to sink.

Peter's response to this episode is surprising. We expect him to jump for joy and this fisherman's windfall; instead, he falls at Jesus' feet and says, *"Depart from me; for I am a sinful man, O Lord"* (Lk. 5:8).

Why would he make such a statement? He seeks to put a distance between himself and the Lord because he feels completely overwhelmed by a sense of mystery. He is uncomfortable in the presence of this one who is sovereign over creation—an "amateur" fisherman whose skill and knowledge of the sea surpassed an "expert" like himself.

There is something mysterious about this man. He is different...distinct...other. His very presence exposed Peter's sin (like the sunlight exposes dust on the furniture) and evoked a sensation of intense anxiety: "Depart from me..." Sinful people are supremely uncomfortable in the presence of sovereign power.

Second, in Luke 5:17-26, Jesus displayed *his sovereign power over disease*. Four men brought their friend—a paralytic—to Jesus for healing. When they could not press through the crowd to Jesus, they climbed the roof and let the palsied man down into the house on a stretcher. When Jesus saw their faith, He forgave the man's sins.

The scribes and Pharisees, however, murmured against Jesus: "Who can forgive sins, but God alone?" But Jesus replied, "Whether is easier, to say, 'Thy sins be forgiven thee'; or to say, 'Rise up and walk'?" Then to demonstrate His authority to forgive sins—an intangible miracle—Jesus said to the paralyzed man, "Arise, and take up thy couch, and go into thine house." Immediately, the man rose and walked—a tangible miracle.

How did the people respond to this One who demonstrated sovereignty over both the external disease of paralysis and the internal disease of sin? Verse twenty-six says, they *"were filled with fear, saying, 'We have seen strange things today'."* They could not fathom such mysterious power.

Third, in Luke 7:11-17, Jesus demonstrated *his sovereign power over death*. As He entered the city of Nain, Jesus met the funeral procession of a young man—a widow's only son. This woman was not only broken hearted by virtue of her son's death, but destitute, for she had lost her sole source of livelihood. Moved with compassion for her, Jesus interrupted the dirge and spoke life to the corpse: "Young man, I say unto thee, 'Arise'. And he that was dead sat up, and began to speak. And he delivered him to his mother" (vs. 14-15).

How did the people at Nain respond to this unique and amazing Man—this One who exercised sovereignty even over death? *"And there came a fear on all..."* (v. 16). They were awestruck in His presence. Never had they encountered anyone who had power over death. His presence stunned them. They were filled with a sense of mystery.

Fourth, in Luke 8:22-25, Jesus demonstrated *his sovereign power over nature*. Sailing to the other side of the sea of Galilee with his disciples, Jesus fell asleep. Suddenly a great storm that threatened the safety of all on board arose. The disciples, panicked and hysterical, awoke Jesus, saying, "Master, master, we perish." Then Jesus rebuked the wind and the sea by a single imperative, "Peace, be still." Immediately, the wind ceased and there was a great calm.

How did the disciples react to this One who had power over the tempest—to this unusual Man who could but speak to the water and it would obey Him? *"And they being afraid wondered, saying one to another, 'What manner of man is this! For he commandeth even the winds and water, and they obey Him'."* (v. 25).

They were perplexed. They could not fathom such foreign and alien power. Though the storm was frightening, Jesus was more frightening still. In the presence of the One who rules the waves, they were struck with a profound sense of mystery.

Finally, in Luke 8:26-39, Jesus demonstrated *his* **sovereign power over people.** In the country of the Gadarenes was a demon-possessed man. He was a terror to himself and to all the citizens of that country. This madman lived in the cemetery, engaged in self-destructive behavior, and behaved like a wild, rabid animal. Society had attempted to restrain him, but the powers that possessed him gave him superhuman strength and he had broken the chains from his hands and feet. When he saw Jesus coming, the demons recognized Jesus (Jas. 2:19). The man fell down to worship Jesus, not in godly fear, but with the fear of dread and punishment: "Torment me not."

Indeed, by society's standards, this wild man was in a hopeless condition. The citizens of Gadara had learned to keep their distance from him. No doubt, they had frequently warned their little ones to avoid him. They took great precautions to protect themselves against this lunatic. But there is not a case too difficult for the Lord. Jesus exorcised the demons, transformed the man, and put him in his right mind. He transformed the man's life.

How did the citizens of Gadara respond when they saw this insane man sitting at Jesus' feet, clothed, and in his right mind? Did they say, "Hallelujah! Praise God! Three cheers for Jesus!"? No, instead, *"they were afraid...then the whole multitude of the country of the Gadarenes round about besought Jesus to depart from them"* (v. 37).

They were frightened by such power. They had never witnessed anything like it before. It made them uncomfortable. They had learned how to deal with this madman—in a sense, they could understand him and live with him. But they could not understand Jesus. How could they live with Him? Traumatized and overwhelmed by His power, they could not bear to be in the presence of Divine Purity.

If we would be God-fearing people, we should cultivate the habit of thinking great thoughts about God. We must regularly meditate on the attributes of God, like His sovereign power, for godly fear, or reverence, arises from right views of the God whose name is "Reverend."

Chapter 9
God's Infinite Majesty

The attitude of reverential awe before God arises not only from a view of His *sovereign power* but also of His *infinite majesty.*

"Majesty" is a familiar theological term employed as a synonym for *glory* and *greatness.* It speaks of God's transcendence—that is, the infinite distance between God and His creatures. He is over, above, and beyond us—"the High and Lofty One that inhabiteth eternity, whose name is Holy" (Is. 57:15). Moses summons all who belong to Jehovah to "ascribe greatness to our God" (Deut. 32:3).

What form does such an ascription of His transcendent majesty take? It employs the grandest and loftiest language available to man: *"The Lord is a great God, and a great King above all gods...The Lord is great, and greatly to be praised: he is to be feared above all gods...For I know that the Lord is great, and the our Lord is above all gods"* (Ps. 95:3; 96:4; 135:5).

So great is God that I am never afraid of exaggeration in my attempt to describe His absolute supremacy and majesty. But still, because our vocabulary is limited, the best that man can do in expressing God's majesty is retreat to the most elementary, childlike language of exclamation, saying simply, "How Great Thou Art!" Indeed, His greatness is unsearchable (Ps. 145:3). In a word, it is "infinite".

Perhaps no chapter concentrates so specifically on the glory and majesty of God as Isaiah 40. Verse nine invites Israel to "Behold" its incomparable God. The prophet then proceeds to display God's inscrutable majesty by showing

His transcendence to everything that man considers to be great.

He is Greater than Nature

Who has not experienced a sense of overwhelming awe at the grandeur of nature? First, the sheer size and power of nature intimidates us. We feel dwarfed and insignificant at the sight of the Grand Canyon, Mt. Everest, or the Pacific Ocean. The power of earthquakes, hurricanes, and tornadoes heighten our sense of frailty and vulnerability. The destructive force latent in the smallest atom makes us tremble in fear.

The immensity and power of God, however, is superior to greatness of nature. He *"measures the waters in the hollow of his hand, and metes out heaven with the span, and comprehends the dust of the earth in a measure, and weighs the mountains in scales, and the hills in a balance"* (v. 12). Commenting on this verse, Jerry Bridges writes, "If a tablespoonful of water in the hollow of my hand represents my holiness, then the waters covering the earth represent God's. If the eight-inch breadth of my hand is a picture of my moral excellence, then the entire span of the universe is a picture of God's."[1]

Though man has not yet invented a telescope powerful enough to explore the farthest reaches of this vast and immense universe, the presence of God pervades it all: *"It is he that sitteth upon the circle of the earth, and the inhabitants thereof are as grasshoppers; that stretcheth out the heavens as a curtain, and spreadeth them out as a tent to dwell in"* (v. 22).

Secondly, the intricate detail and complexity of nature overwhelms us. I know men who have spent their entire adult lives studying the peanut. They would be the first to confess that their knowledge of that obtuse and apparently simplistic plant is only partial. With the invention of the electron microscope, an entirely new scientific discipline known as microbiology and biochemistry has emerged. New discoveries reveal mind-boggling complexity at every level of physiology.

Dr. Francis Crick is credited with the discovery of DNA, the basic building block of life. DNA is a double helix molecule within the nucleus of each of the 30 trillion cells of the human body. Each strand of DNA, if stretched out, would measure about six and one-half feet. If linked together, all the DNA in one human body would reach to the moon and back. Each contains genetic information equivalent to a library of 4000 volumes. Dr. Erwin Lutzer comments, "If we multiply that by 30 trillion [cells], we can begin to appreciate the complexity of a single human being."[2]

Indeed, man is "fearfully and wonderfully made" (Ps. 139:14). The human heart, for instance, weighs only about 10.5 ounces yet pumps non-stop a capacity of 2000 gallons of blood per day for approximately 75 years with the valves opening and closing four to five thousand times per hour. Could man design a pump with this capacity and longevity?

Consider further the incredible wisdom exhibited by insects like the ant or the honey bee. These creatures work with amazing precision to build sophisticated social colonies and precise architectural structures through an elaborate system of communication, organization, and navigational skill that is uncanny.

Still further, consider the amazing variety and beauty of nature. The endless variety of flowers, plants, animals, insects, landforms, etc., is stunning. And the examples could go on and on.

Though the complexity and detail of nature is astounding, God's wisdom is greater still: *"Who hath directed the Spirit of the Lord, or being his counselor hath taught him? With whom took he counsel, and who instructed him, and taught him in the path of judgment, and taught him knowledge, and showed to him the way of understanding?"* (vs. 13-14).

Hidden within the natural creation is a seemingly endless resource of intricate riches and treasures of knowledge (Ps. 104:24). The discipline of exploring and uncovering these intricacies in God's world is true science (Pro. 25:2). The basis of all scientific inquiry is the creation mandate to "subdue the earth and rule over it" (Gen. 1:28)—that is, to discover how the various resources may be used for the benefit of man and the glory of God.

The information and wisdom that men may accumulate from the natural world, however, is not an end in itself. It is intended to lead us to admire the wisdom of the God who created it and to worship Him with an attitude of reverence and godly fear.

Thirdly, the order and integrity of nature fascinates us. Though the universe is incredibly complex, yet each small part functions together in amazing precision. We marvel at the systematic movement of planets, the regularity of the tides, the continuity of the seasons. We stand amazed at the balance of the ecosystems in nature and at the energy sustained by the sun. It continues to function better than the most precise product of human engineering.

Indeed, nature is great. But God is greater. The stability and integrity of nature is due to His maintenance: *"Lift up your eyes on high, and behold who hath created these things, that bringeth out their host by number: he calleth them all by names by the greatness of his might, for that he is strong in power; not one faileth"* (v. 26).

He is Greater than Empires

People also consider political empires and nations to be great, but God is greater and more impressive than the mightiest nation: *"Behold, the nations are as a drop of the bucket, and are counted as the small dust of the balance: behold, he taketh up the isles as a very little thing…All nations before him are as nothing; and they are counted to him less than nothing"* (vs. 15, 17). Whether America, or China, or Russia, or Great Britain—none are a threat to God.

Men are impressed by royalty, but God *"bringeth the princes to nothing; he maketh the judges of the earth as vanity"* (v. 23). Men are impressed by a nation's resources, but *"Lebanon is not sufficient to burn, nor the beasts thereof sufficient for a burnt offering"* (v. 16). All the pomp and circumstance and military might of every nation in the world is like the small dust of the balance before God. He is not intimidated by it. It does not challenge Him. He is not impressed.

He is Greater than Sin

Further, God is greater than sin: *"Speak ye comfortably to Jerusalem, and cry unto her, that her warfare is accomplished, that her iniquity is pardoned: for she hath received of the Lord's hand double for all her sins"* (v. 2). Though the glory of man withers and fades like the flower of the field, the Lord has come with a strong hand and conquered every foe (vs. 6-8, 10). To the man who recognizes the greatness of his sin, the gospel brings *"good tidings"* (v. 9). It proclaims that His grace is greater than all your sin. It cries triumphantly, "The war is over—our iniquities are pardoned!"

He is Greater than Problems

Finally, people often feel overwhelmed by the greatness of their problems. Sometimes they even complain, *"My way is hid from the Lord, and my judgment is passed over from my God"* (v. 27). Indeed, the burdens of life are frequently complicated and foreboding.

But regardless of the magnitude of your problems, God is greater: *"Hast thou not known? Hast thou not heard, that the everlasting God, the Lord, the Creator of the ends of the earth, fainteth not, neither is weary? There is no searching of his understanding"* (v. 28).

Are you weakened by your burdens? Do you feel powerless to solve your problems? *"He giveth power to the faint, and to them that have no might he increaseth strength"* (v. 29). Even when the natural energy and optimism of youth gives way to fatigue and discouragement, yet*"they that wait upon the Lord shall renew their strength; they shall mount up with wings as eagles; they shall run, and not be weary; they shall walk, and not faint"* (vs. 30-31), for God is greater than every problem, and His greatness is unsearchable.

Then, behold your God, my friend, entrust your future into His sovereign hands, and bow before Him in godly reverence, for He is infinite in majesty!

---

[1] Jerry Bridges, *The Joy of Fearing God*, p. 69.
[2] Facts and quotations from D. James Kennedy, Skeptics Answered, pp. 61-63.

Chapter 10
God's Inflexible Justice

"My flesh trembleth for fear of thee; and I am afraid of thy judgments."
- Psalm 119:120

Nahum begins his staggering prophecy with these words against Nineveh: *"God is jealous, and the Lord revengeth; the Lord revengeth, and is furious; the Lord will take vengeance on his adversaries, and he reserveth wrath for his enemies. The Lord is slow to anger, and great in power, and will not at all acquit the wicked..."* (Nah. 1:2-3). So much for easing in to the subject!

Among the attributes of God that are especially suited to the promotion of godly fear, those with a judicial flavor—i.e. His justice, righteousness, and wrath—are most conspicuous. Nothing corrects the popular trend toward religious softness and sentimentality like a review of God's judicial attributes.

Of course, we modern folk tend to react to language like Nahum's with the wince of impropriety. But it is doubtful that talk about Divine judgment was ever very popular.

Why do modern people dislike talk about the justice of God? The subject is rebuffed because we modern folks have lost sight of two very important facts—the absolute holiness of God and exceeding sinfulness of sin. I suspect Nahum's words sound foreign to many professing believers today because they are unaware of the details of Ninevah's history.

The ancient city of Ninevah, together with the entire Babylonian kingdom, was established by Nimrod (Gen. 10:8-12; Mic. 5:6). Approximately 800 years before Christ, Ninevah became the capital of Assyria (modern day

Iran)—a nation known for its wickedness and ruthless violence. Contemporary bible teacher John MacArthur quotes the following description of the climate in ancient Ninevah:

> The Assyrian kings literally tormented the world. They flung away the bodies of soldiers like so much clay; they made pyramids of human heads; they sacrificed holocausts of the sons and daughters of their enemies...they impaled 'heaps of men' on stakes, and strewed the mountains and choked the rivers with dead bones; they cut off the hands of kings, and nailed them on the walls, and left their bodies to rot with bears and dogs on the entrance gates of cities; they...covered pillars with the flayed skins of rival monarchs...and these things they did without sentiment or compunction.[1]

Not long after Jonah prophesied against Ninevah, Sennacherib assumed the Assyrian throne in Ninevah and resumed the history of brutality. In 722 B.C., he attacked the Northern Kingdom of Israel and led the ten tribes into captivity. Then he presumed to attack the Southern Kingdom of Judah under Hezekiah's reign. MacArthur says, "Through Nahum, God was in effect saying He would no longer tolerate the sins of such a nation or the persecution of His people."[2]

Though the prophecy of Jonah depicts God's goodness and mercy, the prophecy of Nahum reminds us of His severity (Rom. 11:22). It corrects the tendency to sentimentalize the kindness of God, balancing that comforting truth with the sobering reminder that ultimately a Holy God must take vengeance on sin.

God had already suffered long with the Ninevites (over 100 years elapsed between Jonah's and Nahum's respective prophecies). He had given ample space for repentance and they had received the benefits of His patience and kindness. Now, in their hardened and impenitent state, His severe judgments were ready to fall. Three great truths emerge from this passage:

Sin Deserves God's Judgment

Everyone who rebels against the authority of his Creator is God's "adversary" and "enemy." "God is jealous," says Nahum. He will not give His glory to another (Is. 42:8); neither will He allow sin—a coming short of His glory (Rom. 3:23)—to go unnoticed. All who chafe against His government incur His wrath and fall under His judgment.

Divine wrath against sin is essential to the holy nature of God. If sin is allowed to go unpunished, the very principle of justice and moral equity loses its meaning. What would happen to a society in which the judge allowed evildoers to walk free? It makes no sense to say that God "loves righteousness" unless He also, on the flip side, "hates unrighteousness" (Heb. 1:8).

Nahum asserts "The Lord revengeth and is furious." The word "furious" speaks of a controlled anger—a fixed disposition. Wrath is the expression of God's settled anger against all who defy Him. God is "angry with the wicked every day" (Ps. 7:11). It is not a temper tantrum, or an irrational outburst of bad temper. No, wrath is not unworthy of God; it is a righteous indignation, a judicial retribution against unholiness.

The New Testament teaches that all men, by nature, are "children of wrath, even as others" (Eph. 2:3). History is marked by ongoing revelations of God's wrath against sin (Rom. 1:18ff) and will conclude with a final "day of wrath, and revelation of the righteous judgment of God" (Rom. 2:5; 2 Ths. 1:8). That day will be a day of "restitution of all things," that is, a time when all wrongs will be made right and all accounts will be settled (Acts 3:21). Believers are people who praise Jesus Christ for the mighty deliverance He has wrought out for them from "the wrath to come" (Rom. 5:9; 1 Ths. 1:10).

Arthur Pink was correct to say that believers should meditate frequently on the wrath of God. First, that our hearts may be duly impressed by God's detestation of sin. Second, to beget a true fear in our souls for God. Third, to draw out our souls in fervent praise for having delivered us from it.[3]

God Does Not Negotiate His Holiness

The passage from Nahum says, "He will not at all acquit the wicked." God is too perfect to slight His holy law by allowing sin to go unpunished. Every disobedience will receive a just recompense of reward (Heb. 2:2).

Many people think that God grades on a curve—that is, He lowers the standard and makes adjustments for human imperfection. But God never extends mercy at the expense of justice. No one will be saved in heaven because he got an "E" for effort. God demands perfection (Ps. 24:3-5) and just one sin is enough to banish a man from God forever (Jas. 2:10). It is not that some men get mercy and others get justice. Whether a man spends eternity in heaven or in hell, justice will be served exactly in every case. The righteous will be saved because Christ satisfied the demands of God's holy law in their stead; the wicked will be judged according to their works (Rev. 20:11-15), but in both cases, justice will be served.

Neither will God negotiate His holiness in providence. He will not simply overlook a sin (Ex. 20:7), even in the lives of His children (Jer. 30:11; Ps. 89:30-33). He will never simply scold the man who sins with a slap on the wrist or a displeased, "Naughty, naughty." He "will by no means clear the guilty" (Ex. 34:7; Jos. 24:19), but will "magnify the law and make it honorable" (Is. 42:21).

God Does Not Give Preferential Treatment

Finally, Scripture teaches that God's justice is impartial. His judgments are not influenced by a man's reputation, family lineage, past performance, social status, or personal giftedness.

God judges "according to every man's work" for there is no respect of persons with Him (1 Pet. 1:17; Deut. 10:17). He does not give preferential treatment to one man above another, but judges each on his own merits (Col. 3:23-25; Eph. 6:9; Rom. 2:6-12; 2 Cor. 5:10). Only the man who "fears God and works righteousness is accepted with Him" (Acts 10:34-35), for that man gives evidence of God's grace in the soul.

How should God's people respond to these sobering truths? Psalm 2 answers "Serve the Lord with fear, and rejoice with trembling. Kiss the Son, lest he be angry, and ye perish from the way, when his wrath is kindled but a little. Blessed are all they that put their trust in him" (vs. 11-12).

In a word, they should respond in godly fear, taking Him seriously, humbling themselves before Him, and walking carefully in His presence every day. Knowing the terror of the Lord, we persuade men (2 Cor. 5:11); knowing His love to sinners in Christ, we are constrained to live unto Him (2 Cor. 5:14-15). This grace gives us the necessary incentive and confidence to serve him with reverence and godly fear (Heb. 12:28).

[1] MacArthur, *The Love of God*, pp. 45-46.
[2] Ibid. p. 60.
[3] Pink, *The Attributes of God*, p. 77.

Chapter 11
God's Pardoning Grace

"But there is forgiveness with thee, that thou mayest be feared."
-     *Psalm 130:4*

Godly fear arises not only from a sense of the severity of God, but also from an awareness of the goodness and graciousness of God: *"Only fear the Lord, and serve Him in truth with all your heart; for consider how great things He hath done for you"* (1 Sam. 12:24).

The godly Christian author Jerry Bridges writes, "There is something about the love of God that should astound us as sinners. His greatness causes us to stand in awe. His holiness lays us prostrate in the dust. His wisdom calls forth our admiration. But His love, rightly understood, causes us to gasp in amazement."[1]

Indeed, the wonder of wonders—the mystery of all mysteries is God's inscrutable grace to sinful people. Against His sovereign power, we feel our weakness and vulnerability. Against His sovereign grace, we feel our unworthiness and depravity—and we wonder, "Why should He love me so?".

Numerous Christian hymns capture this sense of holy wonder and gratitude at the spectacle of pardoning grace:

> I stand amazed at the presence of Jesus the Nazarene;
> And wonder how He could love me,
> A sinner condemned, unclean.
> (Chas. Gabriel)

> Amazing Grace, how sweet the sound,
> That saved a wretch like me;

I once was lost but now am found,
Was blind but now I see.
(John Newton)

———

And can it be that I should gain
An interest in the Savior's blood?
Died He for me, who caused His pain,
For me, who Him to death pursued?
Amazing love, how can it be
That Thou my God should'st die for me!
(Chas. Wesley)

———

Was it for crimes that I have done
He groaned upon the tree?
Amazing pity, grace unknown,
And love beyond degree!
(I. Watts)

———

Upon that cross of Jesus, my eyes at times can see
The very dying form of One who suffered there for me
And from my smitten heart with tears, two wonders I confess,
The wonder of His glorious love, and my unworthiness.
(E. Clephane)

The Cross: A Catalyst for Godly Fear

Each of these hymns suggests the thought that nothing is so effective in the promotion of godly fear in the soul as an understanding of the cross of Christ. It is at the cross, not at Mt. Sinai or in the natural creation, that we view the ultimate display of the character of God.

No other scene in human history presents such a comprehensive portrait of the Divine nature as the cross of Christ. Here we see God's holiness, justice, and wrath upon sin like we've never before seen on the stage of world history. The Deluge in Noah's day, the destruction of Sodom and Gomorrah in Abraham's day, the swift justice executed upon Nadab and Abihu together with the thunder and lightning and earthquakes that attended the giving of the Law in Moses' day – though each of these events reveals a God who hates sin and is serious about holiness, yet none of them could possibly compare to the staggering scene of God's own Son, bruised by the Father as the substitute for sinners (Is. 53:10), treading the winepress of Divine wrath alone and bearing the sins of the entire elect family in His own body on the tree (1 Pet. 2:24). Where is there such a vivid portrait of God-forsakeness as this (Ps. 22:1-3)? Where is there a more graphic demonstration of the exceeding sinfulness of sin than the cross?

The cross also presents the clearest picture in history of the wisdom of God. Of course, God's wisdom is displayed in the natural creation (Jer. 10:12; Ps. 104:24). What wisdom it required to construct the universe, both on the macro level of galaxies, solar systems, and planets, and on the micro level of cells, molecules, and atomic particles! Scientists spend entire lifetimes assimilating bits and pieces of the rich treasures of knowledge that God has hidden in His universe, only to confess in the end, "Lo, these are parts of His ways but how little a portion is heard of Him" (Job 26:14).

But the wisdom of God displayed in the natural world pales in comparison to the wisdom necessary to accomplish redemption. Even the angels are perpetually mesmerized by the ineffable wisdom of God in the plan of salvation (Eph. 3:10).

Further, it is at the cross that the power of God shines most brilliantly. Here, God vanquished every foe and single-handedly won the victory over sin. See the power of Christ exhibited as He cries triumphantly, "It is finished!"

Likewise, the cross displays the love and mercy of God more vividly than every other manifestation of Divine mercy in history. Though the gift of rain, a life companion, a child, good health and other temporal blessings are expressions of God's kindness and grace, yet these blessings are nothing to compare with the grace extended to sinners who deserved His wrath: "...and were by nature children of wrath even as others; but God, who is rich in mercy, for His great love wherewith He loved us, even when we were dead in sins, hath quickened us together with Christ (by grace ye are saved)" (Eph. 2:3b-4; cf. 1 Jno. 4:8-10; Rom. 5:6-8; 2 Cor. 8:9).

Forgiveness: A Catalyst for Godly Fear

Psalm 130:3-4 teaches that, far from promoting licentiousness, God's grace in forgiving our sins leads to godly fear: "If Thou, Lord, shouldest mark iniquities, O Lord, who shall stand? But there is forgiveness with Thee, that Thou mayest be feared."

The individual who reasons that it is permissible to indulge his sinful nature because, "After all, my home in heaven is secure" or "God will forgive me" does not understand either the heinousness of his own sin or the wonder of Divine grace.

Grace, properly understood, is not a license to sin—in fact, it is the greatest incentive to holiness a person will ever know (Titus 2:11-12). The fact that He has forgiven my sins should lead to a holy detestation and hatred of sin in my life: *"Ye that love the Lord, hate evil"* (Ps. 97:10; cf. Pro. 3:7; 16:6; Job 28:28). Could this be the thought in Cowper's mind when he wrote, "I hate the sins that made Thee mourn and drove me from thy breast"?

The late C. H. Spurgeon called the 130th Psalm the "chiefest" and "most excellent" of all the Penitential Psalms. He comments on verse four: "Gratitude for pardon produces far more fear and reverence of God than all the dread which is inspired by punishment...it is grace which leads the way to a holy regard of God, and a fear of grieving Him."[2] Indeed, no one truly loves God unless he is afraid of offending Him.

Forgiveness does not make the pardoned sinner reckless and heedless, but cautious and vigilant against sin: *"The goodness of God leadeth thee to repentance"* (Rom. 2:4); *"Ye repented after a godly sort...what carefulness it wrought in you; yea, what fear..."* (2 Cor. 7:11).

This fear that is excited by grace is a dread, as George Bowen says, lest we "lose one glance of love...[or] one work of kindness...[a] fear to be carried away from the heaven of His presence by an insidious current of worldliness, [a] fear of slumber".[3]

Nothing actuates the praises of God's people like a sense of His pardoning grace. The late Congregationalist pastor, Dr. D. Martyn Lloyd-Jones said, "A Christian is a person who never ceases to be amazed at the fact that he is forgiven. He doesn't take it for granted." Instead, He stands in awe at grace. He never tires to exclaim with the prophet, "Who is a God like unto Thee, that pardoneth iniquity, and passeth by the transgression of the remnant of His heritage? He retaineth not His anger forever, because He delighteth in mercy" (Mic. 7:18). And, taking his cue from this verse, he sings with Samuel Davies,

> Great God of wonders! All Thy ways
> Display the attributes Divine;
> But countless acts of pardoning grace
> Beyond Thine other wonders shine;
> Who is a pardoning God like Thee?
> Or who has grace so rich and free?
>
> In wonder lost with trembling joy,
> We praise the pardon of our God;
> Pardon for crimes of deepest dye,
> A pardon bought with Jesus' blood;
> Who is a pardoning God like Thee?
> Or who has grace so rich and free?
>
> O may this strange, this matchless grace,
> This God-like miracle of love
> Fill the wide earth with grateful praise,
> As now it fills the choirs above!
> Who is a pardoning God like Thee?
> Or who has grace so rich and free?

This good, gracious, and pardoning God has condescended to bestow His favor upon sinful men and women in Christ. What greater incentive to avoid sin, to go softly, to walk humbly, and to pursue holiness may be found than the cross of Christ?

An understanding of God's grace in salvation teaches us to "deny ungodliness and worldly lusts and to live soberly, righteously and godly in this present world" (Titus 2:11-12). It moves us to humble carefulness lest we exhibit by our actions an attitude that scorns the goodness and forbearance of God (Rom. 2:4) and expresses despite to the Spirit of grace (Heb. 10:29).

Who would dare to offend such a loving and gracious God? Far from the popular notion that godly fear is a response fit only for the Holy God that is revealed in the Old Testament, the cross reminds us that it is also the appropriate response for the Gracious God that is revealed in the New. This God, the God of justice and of grace, is the God we love to fear.

---

[1] Jerry Bridges, *The Joy of Fearing God*, p. 97.
[2] Charles Spurgeon, *The Treasury of David*, Vol. II, p. 1164.
[3] Ibid. p. 1173,

Chapter 12
The Blessing of Fearing God

"In the fear of the Lord is strong confidence: and his children shall have a place of refuge. The fear of the Lord is a fountain of life, to depart from the snares of death." Proverbs 14:26-27

Far from the popular notion that views the fear of God as something negative and legalistic, Scripture presents the subject in very positive and affirming terms. The popular caricature of a God-fearing person as one whose brow is perpetually furrowed with a censorious and peevish frown is foreign to the portrait of Divine Inspiration. Instead, God's word teaches that godly fear leads to joyful living.

In Proverbs 14:27, for instance, Solomon asserts, *"The fear of the Lord is a fountain of life"* [lit. a life-giving fountain]. Again he says, in Proverbs 15:16, *"Better is a little with the fear of the Lord than great treasure and trouble therewith"*, and Proverbs 19:23, *"The fear of the Lord lendeth to life: and he that hath it shall abide satisfied; he shall not be visited with evil."* Over and again, blessing is promised to attend the life of the God-fearing person.

In fact, David teaches that God stores up blessings for everyone that fears Him: *"Oh how great is thy goodness, which thou hast stored up for them that fear thee; which thou hast wrought for them that trust in thee before the sons of men! Thou shalt hide them in the secret of thy presence from the pride of man: thou shalt keep them secretly in a pavilion from the strife of tongues"* (Ps. 31:19-20).

Commenting on this passage, Jerry Bridges writes, "God is pictured here like a wealthy person who establishes trust funds for his children to be used after they reach maturity…This is what God does for those who fear Him. He sets aside or stores up goodness for His children, to be given at appropriate times in the future…Even though things may be dark today, God is still storing up goodness for us."[1]

The bottom line of these passages is unmistakable: Scripture promises that the individual who fears the Lord is blessed to enjoy his life in this world with an abiding sense of satisfaction and fulfillment. God's word says to the person who would "love life and see good days" that the road to such earthly blessedness is the path of godly fear (Ps. 34:9-13). Two Psalms—the 112th and the 128th—illustrate this important principle.

Both Psalms open similarly: *"Blessed is the man that feareth the Lord, that delighteth greatly in his commandments'* (Ps. 112:1); *"Blessed is every one that feareth the Lord; that walketh in his ways"* (Ps. 128:1).

The word "blessed" means "happy" and carries the connotation of "success" and "prosperity." The word suggests the thought of inward contentment arising from a general sense of well-being; hence, the Psalmist proceeds to say, *"…happy shalt thou be, and it shall be well with thee"* (Ps. 128:2).

The lovely picture that follows in both Psalms is truly a state or condition that every believer should desire for himself or herself. First, notice the character of a God-fearing person, then four main areas in which the individual who fears the Lord may enjoy a sense of fulfillment.

The Character of the Person who Fears God

The first characteristic of a God-fearing person that emerges from these two Psalms is: A God-fearing individual is marked by a *delightful obedience to God's word*. He "delighteth greatly in His commandments" (Ps. 112:1). He "walketh in His ways" (Ps. 128:1).

A God-fearing person, like his Savior, does God's will joyfully and gladly, not grudgingly and reluctantly (cf. Ps. 40:8). His life is characterized by a steady commitment to righteous behavior (Ps. 112:4).

Secondly, he is *gracious and compassionate to the needy* (Ps. 112:4). This "*good man showeth favor* [lit. *hesed* meaning "lovingkindness; covenant loyalty; mercy; faithful love to the unworthy"] *and lendeth*" (Ps. 112:5). He takes of his substance and gives to the poor (Ps. 112:9a).

Finally, he is *wise and judicious in his business dealings*. He will "*guide his affairs with discretion*" (Ps. 112:5b). The God-fearing person exercises wisdom and integrity in business. He can be trusted for his honesty. He can be consulted for his wise counsel.

All of these things are true of him because he fears the Lord. His life, consequently, is recognized by others with "honor" (Ps. 112:9b) and he is held in reputation and everlasting remembrance for his integrity and righteousness (Ps. 112:6b). What a beautiful picture!

The Blessing of Fulfillment

From these two Psalms we may extract four specific areas in which the person who fears the Lord experiences enjoyment, fulfillment, well-being, and prosperity in life.

First, God promises *a sense of enjoyment and fulfillment in work:* "*For thou shalt eat the labor of thine hands*" (Ps. 128:2a).

Since the Fall of man, the mandate to work has been complicated by sin (cf. Gen. 3:18). Now, work is toilsome labor and mankind is frustrated so that his labor is never completely satisfying. But to the individual who fears the Lord, God promises success and fulfillment in the labor of his hands (cf. Ps. 112:3a).

In other words, God pledges to honor this man's work so that he experiences a certain degree of progress and enjoyment in his labors. Of course, there is nothing wrong with taking pleasure in work: *"I perceive that there is nothing better, than that a man should rejoice in his own works; for that is his portion"* (Ecc. 5:22). But in a special sense, work is more fulfilling to the man who fears the Lord.

In contrast, the individual who does not walk with a holy caution before God, but is dishonest in his dealings with the Lord and others will incur God's judgment and watch as "the work of [his] hands" is dismantled and destroyed (Ecc. 5:6).

Secondly, he experiences *a sense of enjoyment and fulfillment in family life*: *"Thy wife shall be as a fruitful vine by the sides of thine house: thy children like olive plants round about thy table"* (Ps. 128:3). What a lovely scene!

These verses describe the domestic harmony and bliss that attend the life of a God-fearing man: *"Behold, thus shall the man be blessed that feareth the Lord"* (Ps. 128:4).

Again, as a result of Adam's transgression, relationships in the home are typically characterized by strife, tension, rivalry, and disharmony (cf. Gen. 3:16). Men tend toward chauvinistic dominance, women toward self-styled independence, children toward rebellious disobedience, and parents toward the authoritarianism or the abdication of their responsibilities.

The home that was intended to be a haven of rest and affirmation becomes a battleground of conflict. But where the fear of the Lord is present, God honors it so that family life is a very rich and fulfilling part of life. In fact, it is from such God-fearing homes that children grow up to be a mighty influence on others for the Lord's sake (Ps. 112:2).

Thirdly, the man who fears God is promised *the blessing of spiritual fulfillment*: *"The Lord shall bless thee out of Zion: and thou shalt see the good of Jerusalem all the days of thy life"* (Ps. 128:5).

Not only does this individual experience a certain satisfaction from his work and his family, but from his service to the Lord. Seasons spent in the house of God are especially precious to him. God blesses the word to come with power upon his soul. The communion of saints is a sweet cordial in his experience. Public worship is the defining moment of his week. His church life is especially satisfying, for the Lord blesses the God-fearing man out of Zion.

Finally, he experiences *the blessing of emotional fulfillment*: *"He shall not be afraid of evil tidings: his heart is fixed, trusting in the Lord. His heart is established, he shall not be afraid, until he see his desire upon his enemies"* (Ps. 112: 7-8).

There is an emotional stability about his life, because "in the fear of the Lord is strong confidence" (Pro. 14:26). He doesn't live with a lurking fear of hearing "evil tidings" in the back of his mind. He doesn't allow anxiety or discouragement to control his life, for "his heart is fixed, trusting in the Lord."

There is an evenness and steadiness and inner stability that marks his spirit. "His heart is established, he shall not be afraid."

In fact, the God-fearing person enjoys a general sense of well-being: *"Yea, thou shalt see thy children's children, and peace upon Israel"* (Ps. 128:6). In every facet of his life, he senses God's favor and blessing upon him. This is the portrait the Holy Spirit paints of the blessedness of the individual who fears God.

It is an extremely attractive picture, wouldn't you say? May God both kindle the desire for this blessed state in our own lives, and help us to experience the reality of the blessings of fearing God at ever increasing degrees.

---

[1] Jerry Bridges, *The Joy of Fearing God*, pp. 8-9.

Chapter 13
Reverence in Worship

"God is greatly to be feared in the assembly of the saints, and to be had in reverence of all them that are about him." Psalm 89:7

We began this study by talking about our increasingly irreverent culture and the subtle ways that the spirit of this age has influenced popular Christianity. It seems that virtually everywhere, modern churches have jettisoned traditional forms of Divine worship for a more consumer-oriented, seeker-sensitive, and user-friendly "praise experience."

It would be difficult to deny the sheer weight of circumstantial evidence that a basic shift in paradigms, from a God-centered to a more people-centered focus, has taken place over the past thirty years. No longer, it seems, is the primary question "What does God's word say our church should be?" The principal question asked by church leaders today is "What are people looking for in a church? What cultural demographics in the community might we target? What do people want in a church and how can we best meet the demands of the consumer in order to achieve our numerical and financial goals?"

Of course, successful churches are careful to make sure that all is done "in the name of the Lord and with an aim to his honor and glory." But it is hard to escape the sense that the big-business, market-driven, performance-oriented worship model is misdirected.

Would the One who said, "Fear not, little flock, for it is your Father's good pleasure to give you the kingdom" (Lk. 11:32) have felt comfortable with the modern fascination with "numbers and noses"? Would He approve of efforts to cultivate an environment of entertainment? Would He endorse the "give the people what they want" approach to church life?

However we may answer these questions, it is my opinion that the Head of the Church would not appreciate the modern attempts to 'lighten the mood' and to create a more laid-back, casual worship atmosphere. This objective to develop a less-threatening worship environment, and a more conversational, relaxed, non-confrontational and doctrinally-neutral worship experience for the worshipper seems to me to be fundamentally unbiblical and irreverent.

"What does God's word say?" I dare say that question is seldom asked today. Instead, church leaders ask "What do people want?" Relevance, not reverence, is the desired outcome. Relevance...not reverence.

This quest to be relevant to the people—to cater to the popular palate; to accommodate the spirit of this age—is responsible, at a very fundamental level, for the subtle influx of a spirit of irreverence into popular worship. Market-driven church leaders have become increasingly willing to sacrifice reverence for God, the house of God, and the centrality of Scripture on the altar of popularity.

Thus far in this study on "the fear of the Lord," the focus has been on the need to cultivate God-fearing mindsets and lives. In this final chapter, however, let's take the theme to an even more practical level and make specific application of this subject to public worship. When God-fearing people meet together to worship God, the spirit of reverence that characterizes their individual lives should spill over into the assembly.

I believe that rediscovering reverence in worship is one of the great needs of our day. In fact, I maintain that if we want to truly be relevant, we must recapture the God-centered, bible-based model of worship that is revealed in the word of God. Only then may the church be itself, functioning as the Lord designed, and impacting outsiders by its countercultural message and lifestyle.

There is very little that believers in the Lord Jesus Christ can do about the growing spirit of sacrilege and irreverence in society. We do have the ability and the opportunity, however, to work to affect positive change in the church, among people who have already been taught of the Lord via the grace of regeneration to fear him.

Instead of conforming church-life and public worship to a model with which the world is familiar, the gospel church exists in the world by Divine providence for the express purpose of proclaiming a message and modeling a practical ethic that is fundamentally distinct from every other institution. No one else can do the work for which the church was made—not the government, the militia, the schools, the arts, nor the sciences.

Further, in order to maintain its native distinctiveness, the church simply cannot borrow from worldly methods, or allow carnal attitudes to penetrate the congregation. A difference should be evident between the hymn-singing of a church and a rock band, the church's pulpit ministry and a stand-up comic or entertainer, and the spirit of worship and a political rally or music concert.

If there is one place on this earth where reverence for God is still the rule of the day, it should be the church when it meets together for worship. With a view toward encouraging the reader to pursue the rediscovery of reverence in the worship of the church, then, I will offer several suggestions that may prove helpful.

A Sense of God's Presence

Reverence in worship arises *from a conscious sense that we have entered into the presence of the Lord,* not simply the presence of other people. I concur that there is a social element involved in congregational worship. The worship of the church is an opportunity to notice the people around you and to provoke them to love and to good works (Heb. 10:24-25).

But the primary object of attention when the saints gather for public worship should be the Lord. "Enter into His gates with thanksgiving and into His courts with praise," exhorts the Psalmist (Ps. 100:4). Until we have a settled sense that we have entered into His very presence, we should be like a race-horse with blinders, sharpening our focus on Him alone and marginalizing every distraction.

It helps me to remind myself that the name of Zion's city is "The Lord is there" (Eze. 48:35). Though God is omnipresent and, consequently, "not far from every one of us" (Acts 17:27b), yet He has been pleased to choose the church as His special habitation (Eph. 2:22). God "inhabits the praises of His people" (Ps. 22:3). The sweet Psalmist of Israel describes the gracious blessing of public worship in terms of approaching the presence of God: "Blessed is the man whom thou choosest, and causest to approach unto thee, that he may dwell in thy courts: we shall be satisfied with the goodness of thy house, even of thy holy temple" (Ps. 65:4).

John saw the risen and glorified Christ "walking in the midst of the seven golden candlesticks," a symbol of our Lord's active involvement in and presence among His churches. Nothing will prove to be a better help to the cultivation of an environment of reverence in the worship of the church than the discipline of consciously thinking as I sit in the pew, "I am in the presence of the great God of heaven."

Hearing God's Word

It is further helpful to *check your attitude toward God's word*. Ask yourself the question, "Is my heart tender and humble so that I might receive God's word? Am I eager to hear what the Lord has to say to me through His servant today?"

Reverence in worship is a by-product of the individual worshipper's conscious awareness that God still speaks through what He has already spoken in Scripture. "Today, if you will hear His voice," says the Holy Spirit, "harden not your hearts" (Heb. 3:7-8). Though it is an ancient word that we speak, it is a contemporary message, with up-to-the-minute relevance to our lives.

James urges believers to do certain preparatory work before public worship begins, so that they may be in a mindset to receive the word: "Wherefore lay apart all filthiness and superfluity of naughtiness, and receive with meekness the engrafted word, which is able to save your souls" (Jas. 1:21)

Receive with meekness" means "approach God's word with a submissive, soft, and pliable spirit." The "rebel sigh" that is native to every person by nature—that natural attitude that proudly resists being told what to do—must be subdued if we are to receive the benefits that are available in the hearing of God's word.

Reverent worship involves hearing the word "as the word of God, not as the word of men" (1 Ths. 2:13). We are not simply hearing the pastor's weekly sermon. We are listening to God.

"We come to hear Jehovah speak, to hear the Savior's voice;
Thy face and favor, Lord we seek; Now let our hearts rejoice."
- Joseph Hoskins

Reverence before the word, then, means that we make a deliberate effort to pray with Samuel as we come to the hour of worship, "Speak, Lord, for thy servant heareth" (1 Sam. 3:9). It means that we come with the eagerness of Cornelius: "We are all here present before God, to hear all things that are commanded thee of God" (Acts 10:33b).

When Ezra the scribe opened God's word at the rededication of the walls of Jerusalem, the people spontaneously "stood up" and remained standing as he read (Neh. 8:5). The spontaneity of their reaction speaks of their deep reverence and sense that they were about to hear something of sacred and Divine significance.

Such spontaneity cannot be scripted or coerced. When the preacher invites the people to stand up out of respect for the word, it somehow loses the effect.

The story is told that during the virgin performance of Handel's celebrated oratorio *Messiah*, King George II and his court suddenly stood to their feet as the composition reached the climactic point of the "Hallelujah Chorus." So moved was the king by the rising action of "Comfort Ye My People," "To Us a Child is Born," and "A Virgin Shall Conceive," that he spontaneously rose to his feet when the prophecies reached the long-awaited crescendo at Messiah's incarnation and victory.

That same sensation should pervade our hearts as we wait with abated breath for a word from God each Lord's day. As a preacher, I do not seek the endorsement from my auditors, "You had a nice sermon this morning, pastor." I had much rather hear, "What a powerful word from the living God today!"

It will also help you to hear the word reverently to make preparations for public worship in advance. Most people are like an old lawnmower that I owned. The lawnmower required a dozen jerks on the pull-cord before it cranked. But if I primed the carburetor in advance, the engine would start on the first pull.

Have you ever sat in a mental and spiritual fog through an entire worship service, only to find the mist begin to lift, and the frost on your spirit begin to thaw, as the benediction was said? How much better it would be to take time to pray for the service in advance, to read from the Bible and listen to Christian hymns! The spiritual discipline of preparing to worship the Lord will generally serve to "prime the pump" so that available blessings in the house of God are not missed.

Behaving Reverently in the House of God

Finally, a word needs to be said about how to behave ourselves in public worship (1 Tim. 3:15). When it comes to maintaining an atmosphere conducive to the serious act of Divine worship, liturgical traditions do not seem to have as much of a challenge as free traditions.[1]

Those of us who favor freedom in worship would argue that joy is a fruit of the Holy Spirit and that the more liturgical traditions tend to quench the Spirit by stifling the kind of celebratory tone that is exhibited in the worship scenes of the books of Acts and Revelation. It is a valid argument.

Who wants a sanitized, rote, and formal worship in which people are afraid to say "Amen" or shed a tear of joy while the gospel is proclaimed? Godly fear, as we have previously noted, is not a kind of paralysis in which people are afraid to move. When the leadership of the church develops such a stiff and perfectionistic worship environment that people are afraid to rejoice in the Lord or sing out loud for fear of hitting a wrong note, the very meaning of "worship" has been lost. "Where the Spirit of the Lord is, there is liberty" (2 Cor. 3:17b).

Reverence does not mean that it is inappropriate to smile, or for a preacher to weave some discretionary humor into the sermon for the sake of making a point and engaging the congregation. God's people should be a happy people (Ps. 144:15) and happy people are likely to express their gladness of heart. A woman once said of George Whitefield that even though she did not understand all of the nuances of his theology, yet she wanted to know more because anything that could make a person that happy was something she wanted for herself.

I am confident that the Lord does not disapprove of momentary laughter in the worship service. C. H. Spurgeon once defended himself against a critics charge of levity in the pulpit by saying, "I think it a lesser crime to cause momentary laughter than half-an-hour of profound slumber." But in our quest to worship freely, it is important to avoid the kind of childish silliness in which the preacher becomes a stand-up comic and the service, a spectacle in entertainment.

Most reasonable people would likely agree, in other words, that "freedom" is not an absolute concept. There is no such thing as freedom from every restraint. The locomotive is free so long as it stays on the rails. Outside of the context of the train rails, however, it won't get very far.

Many folks would also agree (I suspect) that a number of the groups in the free-worship tradition have taken the concept of freedom in worship to an extreme. No doubt, the reader has witnessed worship services that began reverently enough, only to turn into a chaotic free-for-all of emotional outbursts by the time it was over.

Chaos in public worship was one of the problems in the church at Corinth, as described in 1 Corinthians 14. Evidently, different believers, male and female alike, were standing up simultaneously to showcase their respective spiritual gifts. The effect was that they were talking over each other and feeling offended that someone else had taken their spotlight. It was pandemonium.

Paul urges them to think of how their behavior might appear to a visitor: "If...there come in those that are unlearned, or unbelievers, will they not say that ye are mad?" (1 Cor. 14:23). Paul knows that drastic maladies call for drastic measures, so he places a moratorium on speaking[2] on the females in the church, saying, "If you have questions, then wait until you get home and ask your husbands" (vs. 34-35). He urges the "prophets," or preachers, to make pulpit arrangements (v. 32), and to limit that to "two, or at the most, three" preachers in sequence during a particular service (v. 29).

He reminds them that God is not the author of confusion, but of peace (v. 33), and concludes his counsel with an exhortation to orderliness: "Let all things be done decently and in order" (v. 40). Obviously, Paul did not approve (nor did the Holy Spirit who inspired Paul to write 1 Cor. 14) of the irreverent climate that the Corinthian Church had allowed to develop in their worship of the Lord.

Folks who are accustomed to people dancing, fainting in the aisles, waving arms, glossalalia, pew jumping, ecstatic utterances, holy laughter, and the rest are convinced that this kind of highly-emotional environment is a manifestation of the Spirit of God. An argument could be made, however, that a hyper-active atmosphere in any gathering of people—whether it be a rock concert, a political rally, a pagan ritual, a school pep-rally, or a religious worship service—may be psychologically induced and manipulated.

If people have been taught to think of Christian worship as primarily an emotional experience in which they feel a kind of spiritual high, then come to worship expecting such a display as the norm, or regular fare, in church life, then it only takes a medley of praise choruses, a certain cadence and tonal inflection from the worship leader, and the audience is worked up to a spiritual frenzy.

Of course, excesses like I have cited do not negate the fact that emotions and feelings are an integral part of who we are as human beings and occupy a valid place in discipleship. It is important to note, especially for those of us who are convinced that true worship involves not only doctrine, but also devotion—not only the head, but also the heart (Jno. 4:24)—that the fruit of the Spirit is not only joy, but temperance, or self-control (Gal. 5:22-23).

The loss of self-control is not a proof that the Holy Spirit is present. In fact, the opposite is true. Where the Spirit of God is present, the grace of temperance (as well as the virtue of joy) is evident.

I believe it is possible to enjoy freedom in worship without sacrificing reverence, and, on the flip side, to cultivate an environment of holy seriousness without the loss of joy. I suspect, however, that the need of the hour among those of us who subscribe to the free-worship model is greater seriousness and reverence, not greater freedom of expression.

Rediscovering reverence in church worship begins as individual members make the effort to be as prompt as possible and arrive on time. It is so easy to slip into a habit of leaving too late and straggling into the sanctuary just a few moments prior to the preaching part of the service.

Every time I have attended a symphony performance, or a play, or a concert, I've noticed that an effort is made to keep folks that arrive late from entering the auditorium until there is a break in the action. Showing respect to the performers on stage and the other auditors is an ethical given—an unwritten rule understood by all—in that environment.

The same kind of effort to arrive in a timely fashion should be made when it comes to the worship service. If the orchestral conductor deserves what my grandparents called "simple, old-fashioned, good manners," then the God of heaven certainly does.

When you arrive, please consider sitting close to the front of the building. The back rows of the sanctuary should be kept for visitors and folks who may not yet feel comfortable in the venue. I wonder sometimes if folks that sit on the back pew, while pews in the middle and to the front of the sanctuary remain largely vacant, even consider the not-so-subtle message this sends to visitors, and to the pastor. Though it may not be intentional, the habit says, "I'm not that interested in what is going on here. I don't want to get too involved. I prefer to keep my distance. I reserve the right to make a quick get-a-way."

Personally speaking, I want to be where the action is. I like to sit as closely to the front as possible, simply because I don't want to miss anything, or be distracted by what may be going on behind me.

I know that physical posture is not always a barometer of spiritual devotion. God looks on the heart, not the outward appearance. But doesn't he also place a premium on zeal and enthusiasm? Isn't there something to be said for being an encouragement to your pastor that you are sufficiently interested in the word of God so as to arrive on time, to take a seat that shows your desire to be involved, to sit up straight, to participate in the singing, and to listen attentively to God's word? Wouldn't such a change of habit be helpful toward a rediscovery of reverence in the worship of the local church?

In the spirit of rediscovering reverence in our worship of God, I would also exhort you to try to cut to a minimum leaving the sanctuary during the service. I've been in worship services in which there was a steady stream of folks getting up to go to the restroom, then coming back in five or ten minutes later.

I recognize that there are people who have physical problems. But when the same folks get up every service, just ten or fifteen minutes into the sermon and stay gone for a quarter of an hour, one begins to wonder if they are sensitive to the level of distraction to the congregation and the preacher it is, not to mention the fact that they have just missed a significant part of the sermon.

Of course, mothers or fathers whose children are behaving disruptively should quickly carry them out, discipline them, then bring them back into the service. But it is hard for me to believe that habitual and incessant exiting and entering is healthy to the worshipper himself, considerate of the rest of the congregation, or respectful to the Lord.

Would it not be possible to sit still for an hour to an hour and a half if people planned to take care of physical needs in advance? I suspect most people are able to sit through a two-hour movie at the theater or a three-hour ballgame without leaving the venue. God and your fellow believers deserve at least the same level of consideration.

We might also talk about the need to be amply rested so that one is able to stay awake during the service, or to silence cell phones or, better yet, leave them in the car. Young people should be taught by their parents that text messaging during the worship service is unacceptable behavior. Older folks should know, simply by means of common sense and old-fashioned good manners, that you certainly don't answer a ringing cellular phone during the worship of God.

Of course, none of these matters can be legislated without sliding precariously into legalism. There will be caveats and exceptions when folks forget, or experience a physical need, or unwittingly fall asleep because the Saturday-afternoon preacher is talking in a monotone about the intricate details of the offering of the red heifer. Everyone with reasonably good sense and patience toward human imperfections understands such matters.

My point is that we, as people who have come to offer the sacrifice of worship and praise to the God of heaven, should make a deliberate effort to show reverence and holy respect to God as the rule in our churches. No doubt, each of us could improve in this area.

The hymnwriter Isaac Watts put it poignantly:

> With reverence let the saints appear
> And bow before the Lord;
> His high commands with reverence hear
> And tremble at His word.
> How terrible Thy glories be!
> How bright Thine armies shine!

> Where is the power that vies with Thee,
> Or truth compared with Thine?
> The northern pole and southern rest
> On Thy supporting hand;
> Darkness and day from east to west
> Move round at Thy command.

The God we worship is, indeed, a great and sovereign God. He rules the universe. He commands the armies of heaven. He speaks to us in His word. This God, therefore, is "greatly to be feared"—that is, taken seriously, humbly adored, and deeply respected—"in the assembly of the saints and to be had in reverence among all them that are about Him."

---

[1] Liturgical worship is generally highly-structured and scripted, while free worship is characterized by a minimum of structure. Examples of the former would include Catholics, Anglican/Episcopalians, and Presbyterians. Examples of the latter include Baptists, Methodists, and Pentecostals.

[2] First Timothy 2:12 is the official, or policy, position concerning the role of women in public worship. There, Paul insists (in language that would be difficult to misunderstand) that females are prohibited from occupying a "teaching," or leadership, role in the church. It seems that 1 Corinthians 14:34 is not so much a procedural, but a remedial, solution to the particular problems at Corinth. Here he uses a more comprehensive term than the 1 Timothy passage, forbidding the women even to "speak." Those who interpret 1 Cor. 14:34 in terms of church polity face the uncomfortable position of having to defend any verbal involvement of females in the worship of the church, even participation in the verbal singing of hymns or giving a verbal confession of faith at baptism.

www.ingramcontent.com/pod-product-compliance
Lightning Source LLC
Chambersburg PA
CBHW020916090426
42736CB00008B/658